D0831805

CULTURE SMART!
NEW ZEALAND

Sue Butler and Ljiljana Ortolja-Baird

·K·U·P·E·R·A·R·D·

ISBN 978 1 85733 856 0
This book is also available as an e-book: eISBN 978 1 85733 857 7
British Library Cataloguing in Publication Data
A CIP catalogue entry for this book is available from the British Library

First published in Great Britain
by Kuperard, an imprint of Bravo Ltd
59 Hutton Grove, London N12 8DS
Tel: +44 (0) 20 8446 2440   Fax: +44 (0) 20 8446 2441
www.culturesmart.co.uk
Inquiries: sales@kuperard.co.uk

Series Editor Geoffrey Chesler
Design Bobby Birchall

Printed in Malaysia

About the Authors

SUE BUTLER is an English writer who lived and worked in New Zealand for three years. After gaining two Honors degrees, in Philosophy and Psychology, she worked in advertising, public relations, and crisis management, coauthoring a book on the subject. She has been a journalist and magazine editor, and has managed her own PR company. While in New Zealand Sue contributed to several magazines, and traveled widely throughout the country. She and her husband now live in the wine-growing region of the Western Cape in South Africa.

LJILJANA ORTOLJA-BAIRD has an M.A. from the University of London. She has worked as an editor and publisher with several major publishing houses, most recently with the Hachette group. Her publishing associations with New Zealand authors consolidated her keen interest in the country that developed while an undergraduate student in Australia. Currently based near Cambridge in the UK, she is the editor of the *IMCoS Journal* and assistant editor of *Imago Mundi*, both dedicated to the study of the history of cartography.

The Culture Smart! series is continuing to expand.
For further information and latest titles visit
www.culturesmart.co.uk

contents

contents

Map of New Zealand

introduction

New Zealand, or Aotearoa (the "land of the long, white cloud") as it is known by the Maori population, is a land of myth and reality, contrast and contradiction, rolling hills and glacial mountains, native bush and gentle farmland. Turquoise lakes, fast-flowing rivers, boiling mud, and leaping geysers add drama to the landscape, as do its unique flora and fauna.

New Zealand's culture is rich and diverse because of the numbers of people of different nationalities who have immigrated to the country. Britain's position as the main source country, which it held since early settlement in the nineteenth century, has been superseded variously in the intervening years by China, the Philippines, and India. It is still greatly influenced by its Maori heritage and today it is recognized as part of New Zealand's identity. With this has come an increasing usage of Maori words and phrases in daily life. If you learn a few key words of *te reo Māori* (Maori language) your efforts will be appreciated.

The New Zealanders are a friendly and welcoming people, who will go the extra mile to help you without expecting anything in return. As a nation of immigrants, they themselves have blended to form a unique persona, the Kiwi, who is used to newcomers and will be happy to accept you at face value. Kiwis are usually polite, gentle (off the playing field), trusting, and honest. They are also unpretentious, and are not impressed by airs and graces, preferring a more down-to-earth attitude.

This comes from their roots in the early settler days, when men labored long and hard to "earn a crust," and luxuries were few. A memory of those early times remains, particularly in rural areas and among the older generation who did not have it so easy. So you will find that while Kiwis work to live and improve their lot, they don't need much to keep them content. Sir Edmund Hillary—brave and pragmatic—is repeatedly held up as embodying the spirit of New Zealand. He is quoted as saying: "In some ways I believe I epitomise the average New Zealander. I have modest abilities, I combine these with a good deal of determination, and I rather like to succeed."

New Zealanders feel a strong bond with their natural environment. The recent rescue from sale into private ownership of the Awaroa beach (800 meters of pristine coastline) in the Abel Tasman National Park is testament to their firmly-held opinion that the land should be accessible to all. Forty thousand donors pledged, through a crowd-funding project "Givealittle," more than NZ $2 million toward the cause; and won.

Its moderate climate, clean and green environment, reliable public services, and general safety make it an easy country to visit. *CultureSmart! New Zealand,* while providing factual background information, explores the human dimension, offering tips and vital insights into Kiwi customs, values, and attitudes to help deepen your experience of this country and its fair-minded people.

Key Facts

Official Name	New Zealand	Member of the British Commonwealth
Capital City	Wellington	
Major Cities	Auckland, Christchurch, Hamilton, Dunedin	
Area	103,736 sq. miles (268, 675 sq. km.)	
Geography	New Zealand lies in the SW Pacific, SE of Australia. There are two main islands, the warmer North Island (NI) and the more rugged South Island (SI). The terrain is mainly mountainous.	NI has three active volcanoes, geysers, hot springs, Lake Taupo, and the Waipoua Forest. SI has the Southern Alps, the Canterbury Plains, and fiords in the southwest.
Climate	Temperate, with moderate to abundant rainfall	Summer Dec.–Feb., Winter June–Aug.
Currency	NZ Dollar	
Population	4,664,767 (2016)	Most people live on the North Island.
Ethnic Makeup	European 74%, Maori 15%, Asian 12%, Pacific Peoples 7%, other 1% (2013 census)	"Other" includes Middle Eastern, African and Latin Americans.
Official Language	English and Maori. Maori is spoken by 157,110 people and there is a conscious effort to keep it alive. NZ citizens can request to be addressed in Maori in a court of law. Samoan is the next most common language, spoken by approx. 80,000 people.	

Religion	More than 50% of the pop. is Christian, with Anglicans the largest group (15%), followed by Catholics (12%), Presbyterians (11%), and others.	There are two indigenous Maori religions. Islam, Hinduism, and Buddhism number approx. 50,000. Judaism has been in the country since 1800s.
Government	Parliamentary democracy with a constitutional monarchy	Queen Elizabeth II, the Head of State, is represented in NZ by the Governor General. Seat of government is Wellington.
Media	Three major free to air TV channels; Sky Digital available to subscribers; many local TV stations as well as Maori TV. Over 200 radio stations	23 newspapers are published daily and over 50 locally published magazines.
Electricity	230 volts, 50 Hz	As Australia. 2 or 3 angle-pronged plugs are used. Adaptors are readily available for overseas appliances.
TV/Video	PAL B/G	
Internet Domain	.nz	
Telephone	Country code 64	To dial out, dial 00.
Time Difference	GMT + 12 hrs	Daylight saving from late September to early April, when time is GMT + 13 hrs

chapter one

LAND & PEOPLE

GEOGRAPHICAL SNAPSHOT

New Zealand is situated approximately 994 miles (1,600 km) off the southeast coast of Australia, across the Tasman Sea. Its landmass is slightly bigger than that of the UK—approximately 103,738 square miles (268,680 sq. km), while its population is just over four and half million compared to the UK's sixty-three million. Put another way, in New Zealand there are only sixteen people to the square kilometer, whereas in the UK there are well over 260 (2013).

Although the two main islands, the North and the South, are well known, the country is in fact an archipelago with over 700 offshore islands, most of which are very small and within about 31 miles (50 km) of the coast. The North and the South Islands are long and narrow, stretching from latitude 34° degrees to 47° south. Thus the maximum distance to the sea from any one point is never more than about 80 miles (130 km), and it is the mighty Pacific Ocean that laps the shores of the 10,000–11,000 miles (15,000–18,000 km) of coastline. Due south of the mainland, as the South Island is often called by New Zealanders, is Stewart Island, or Rakiura, which is about 648 square miles (1,680 sq. km) in area. Around 500 miles (850 km) to the east are the Chatham Islands, which, lying just west of the International Date Line, are the first to see the sun rise, and to greet the New Year.

New Zealand's landscape is diverse—from green, gently rolling, sheep-scattered hills in the North Island to dramatic, snowcapped, rocky mountains and lakes in the South. The two main islands are only about 12 miles (20 km) apart, but early visitors felt they were visiting two different countries. Much of the "winterless" far north's hill country is farmed, although there is a lot of forest cover in the higher areas, which rise to nearly 5,600 feet (1,700 meters).

In the center of the island, surrounding Lake Taupo, are a number of volcanoes that have been active for over a million years, while nearby, to the east, are the mud pools and geysers of Rotorua, one of New Zealand's foremost attractions.

The South Island is vast, bigger and chillier than the North, and is divided lengthways by the Southern Alps, the highest point of which is Mount Cook at 12,313 feet (3,753 meters). Lush rain forests lie to the west,

and to the east, where rivers flow from the mountains, lie the extensive farmlands of the Canterbury Plains, which seem to stretch forever. To the south are a number of icy, unbelievably turquoise lakes. This picture-book color is a natural phenomenon caused by the incessant friction of ice and water, which grind the pieces of rock into "rock flour," the tiny floating particles of which help to reflect light. Different again is Stewart Island, which, unlike the North and South Islands, is mostly covered in lush native vegetation on its gentle, rolling hills.

Most of New Zealand's coastline is rocky, but it has a number of bays and harbors around which New Zealanders and visitors love to sail, particularly on the safer eastern waters around the Bay of Islands, where the many islands form a natural protection against the ocean.

Volcanoes and Earthquakes

Not without justification is New Zealand referred to as "the shaky isles." An average year will see thousands of quakes, but only about two hundred will be felt. Volcanic activity occurs mostly in the north, although ancient craters follow a line through the country to islands in the sub-Antarctic nearly 1,000 miles (1,600 km) away.

It must not be forgotten that New Zealand, which was once part of the massive continent Gondwana and separated from Australia around eighty million years ago, is located on the edge of tectonic plates, known as the Pacific "rim of fire." Volcanic activity has given the country its geological history of rising and collapsing mountains, landslides, and the formation of lakes. The Southern Alps, for instance, arose as a result of two huge plates on the Alpine fault meeting and sliding past each other. Most volcanic activity in New Zealand, in the last 1.6 million years, has occurred in the Taupo Volcanic Zone (TVZ). The zone extends from White Island to Ruapehu. On a world scale it is an extremely active area and includes three frequently erupting cone volcanoes (Ruapehu, Tongariro/Ngauruhoe, White Island), and two of the most productive calderas in the world: Okataina and Taupo.

Mount Ruapehu, has been erupting regularly since 1969. The 1996 eruption produced over seven million tons of ash, which could be seen by satellite and affected visibility so badly that air traffic was disrupted.

White Island's volcano, which lies 30 miles (nearly 50 km) off the Bay of Plenty on the eastern side of the North Island, is still active and has an alert level of 1, indicating that it is always steaming; a plume of white smoke issuing from its peak can be seen from the coast. Visitors to the island don hard hats and masks and can view the sulfur works, long abandoned.

Such activity, of course, raises the ugly threat of tsunamis—a word that became familiar to the rest of the world after the tragic Boxing Day tsunami of 2004 in Southeast

Asia, but one that is well understood in this region. New Zealand suffers very large earthquakes every few hundred years, and it is thought that in the fifteenth century a tsunami over 33 feet (10 meters) in height devastated many Maori coastal settlements. In September 2010 a powerful earthquake with a magnitude of 7.1 hit the Canterbury region in the South Island. Six months later a resulting aftershock badly destroyed Christchurch, the island's largest city, killing 185 people.

CLIMATE

"Long on mud and rain" is the perception of New Zealand's climate, and this is not altogether inaccurate. Auckland is estimated to have twice as much rain as London, but also twice as much sun! With seasons reversed from most of the rest of the world, New Zealand's summer is a good time for northern hemisphere dwellers to visit, during their winter. February is usually considered the most stable month for warm weather.

New Zealand lies approximately halfway between Antarctica and the Tropics—"roaring forties" territory, that is often the bearer of winds and stormy seas. The west coast suffers much worse weather than the east, and is less populated as a consequence. The country's climate is officially "cool to temperate," but this leaves out a great deal in between. It is subject to a lot of high and low fronts, and to say the weather is unpredictable is putting it mildly. There is a saying in Auckland, "If you don't like the weather, wait ten minutes."

Temperatures rarely exceed 86°F (30°C), and fall below freezing only in the higher, inland areas and in severe winters in the south, when gales can be forceful, although they also bring the snow to the ski fields. Summer temperatures are between 70 and 75°F (21–24°C) in Auckland, and two or three degrees lower in Queenstown and Christchurch. Winter averages are around 57°F (14°C) in the north, while Queenstown falls to 46°F (8°C) or even lower.

The seasons are discernible, with spring from September to November. Summer, from December to February, is milder in the south and warmer in the north, although Christmas Day can still be unpredictable even though it is officially in summer. Fall, from March to May, can often extend to an Indian summer in the far north while winter, from June to August, brings the rain in the north and snow in the south. It is not unknown, however, for all four seasons to be experienced in one day!

Probably in greater supply than sunshine is rainfall, which can vary from nearly 12 inches (300 mm) annually in Northland to over 236 inches (6,000 mm) on the southwest coast around the Milford Sound. Averages, though, are in the region of 24–59 inches (600–1,500 mm) per annum, although certain areas achieve around 98 inches (2,500 mm). A record-breaking annual rainfall of around 710 inches (over 18,000 mm) was once measured on the west coast at Cropp River.

Most of New Zealand enjoys over 2,000 hours of sunshine a year, with favored spots being the north of the South Island around Nelson and Blenheim, and the east of the North Island, in particular Whakatane, the Bay of Plenty, and Napier. These areas usually exceed 2,350 hours, and even the rainy west coast has around 1,800 hours. However, sunbathers need to be very careful, as the breaks in the ozone layer in the Antipodes are severe, and Auckland has the highest rate of melanoma in the world. Weather forecasts always include references to the burn factor and the length of time one can safely stay in the sun. It is even a regulation that schoolchildren bring hats to play outside. No hat, no play!

A NATION OF ISLANDERS

New Zealand is a multicultural nation, and—as nearly three-quarters of the population is of European, mostly British, origin, with Maori representing approximately 15 percent and the Pacific peoples 7 percent—it can be said to be a nation of islanders. (In comparison, Aborigines represent only 1.8 percent of the population of Australia.) The families of Pacific origin were from Samoa, with the next largest group from the Cook

Islands, then Tonga. Many of today's "Islanders" were born in New Zealand, and far more Cook Islanders, Niueans, and Tokelauans now live in New Zealand than on their own home islands. The Island population is a young one, which lives mostly in the Auckland area.

One in seven New Zealanders claim Maori ethnicity—an increase of 21 percent since 1991, as there are more Maori births than European or Asian. There are, however, no purebred Maoris left. Blood count is no longer a definition, and the term "Maori" now describes a person of that race or a descendant of any such person. The word, which means "normal" or "ordinary" in Maori, came to be used by the incoming Europeans in order to differentiate Maori from other Polynesian tribes who did not identify themselves by a collective name. Maori refer to themselves as *tangata whenua*, which means "people of the land." New Zealand's Asian population amounts to approximately 12 percent of the total, of which the largest group is Chinese, followed by Indians.

The country has changed considerably from its early British and Maori origins and, although this heritage is still evident today, the population is gradually becoming less European. Nearly 20 percent of all children under the age of fifteen are of more than one ethnic group, and half of these have European-Maori parentage. A further change is that the Maori population is younger (only 3 percent are over sixty-five) than the general population (12 percent over sixty-five).

By and large, the different peoples in New Zealand's melting pot live well together. However, Maori and the Pacific Islanders do not enjoy the same living standards as other groups, particularly the Europeans. This, along with poorer health, lower life expectancy, and lower educational achievement, often leads to lower income levels and greater unemployment among their number. Despite some improvement made to address these issues by the last Labour government, a new study from the Victoria University of Wellington shows that inequality has worsened over the last ten years for both Maori and Pacific people. Many of the problems arose when the Maori, a largely rural population until the mid 1900s, had to make the transition to urban living, particularly after the Second World War. From 1951 to 1971, the percentage of Maori coping with city life rose from 20 to 58, and by 2001 Maori were as likely as the rest of the population to be living in cities or larger towns. Recognizing that problems could ensue with two very different cultures living in such close proximity, in 1971 the government appointed a race relations conciliator, now part of the Human Rights Commission.

Recent years have seen a resurgence of Maori identity, with many becoming more vociferous about their loss of land and economic hardship, believing that the 1840 Treaty of Waitangi had been breached. This was the treaty, signed by representatives of the English Crown and various Maori chiefs from the North Island, by which the Maori ceded sovereignty to Britain in return for the rights and privileges of British subjects and the undisturbed possession of their lands. In

1975 a special Tribunal was set up to consider Maori land claims. There are currently more than eight hundred under consideration, and it took the previous government two and a half years to settle two. Part of the problem has been the differences in interpretation of the English and Maori texts of the 1840 Treaty. The process is occupying a team of lawyers full-time and has become big business, leading many MPs to call for a deadline for claims submissions.

A consequence of the Maori cultural renaissance, which came at a time when more immigrants were arriving, was the increased awareness that New Zealand is a multicultural society, with regard not only to its nationalities but also to the way these contributed to an identifiable, national lifestyle, which seemed to have shaken off the European cultural and economic fetters. The Asian population, too, two-thirds of which live in the Auckland area, has had its share of problems, and has often been the target of anti-immigrant feelings. By and large, though, the many groups are welcomed by New Zealanders, who recognize the importance of injecting new blood into their country. By comparing population growth figures of the various ethnic groups in the 2006 and 2013 censuses, the Asian population is predicted to outnumber those of Maori ethnicity.

A BRIEF HISTORY
The Early Days
New Zealand is short on human history—shorter than any other country, as it was the last landmass

in the world to be settled, although the actual date of
settlement is still a matter of conjecture. Maori are
considered to have been the first arrivals, coming
from East Polynesia in the thirteenth century, the
navigator Kupe being credited with discovering the
country. However, the peace-loving Moriori tribe may
have arrived at the same time or earlier, probably also
from Polynesia, as they share similar ancestry with
the Maoris, although their origins are obscure. They
made their home on the Chatham Islands, having
migrated from the South Island. It is believed that there
were more than two thousand Moriori living on the
Chatham Islands in the eighteenth century, but their
numbers were severely depleted by disease and Maori
attacks. Today no one from this gentle tribe is left, the
last full-blooded Moriori having died in 1933.

Maori descendants trace their ancestry back to a
fleet of canoes from Hawaiki, thought to be in the
Society Islands, now called Tahiti. As much of New
Zealand's history dates from preliterate times, myth
and legend have become intertwined with fact, so it
is often difficult to separate the two, or to know when
history takes over from, or replaces, tradition. Maori
legend says that the North Island was fished out of the
sea by Maui, a demigod, hence the Maori name for
the North Island is Te Ika a Maui ("the Fish of Maui").
Concerned that the gods might be angry about this,
Maui went to make peace, leaving his brothers to argue
about ownership of this new land. Their arguments
turned to blows, and their pounding of the catch, or
land, helped to create the mountains and valleys of the
North Island. Similarly, the South Island is known as Te

Waka a Maui ("Maui's Canoe"), and Stewart Island Te Punga a Maui ("Maui's Anchor").

The First Europeans

New Zealand was first sighted by Europeans in 1642, by the Dutch navigator Abel Janszoon Tasman, founder of Tasmania, on his great "South Land" expedition to ascertain if "Terra Australis Incognita" actually existed. It is thought that a Dutch cartographer gave New Zealand its present name because as Australia was then called New Holland, it was appropriate to name the new land after the other main province of the Netherlands, Zeeland.

This southern continent had eluded explorers for centuries, and consequently had gained a reputation for being rich. It was the west coast of the South Island that Tasman saw and charted but, because the first encounter between Maori and Europeans off the coast resulted in the deaths of four Dutchmen, New Zealand was left to its "savage" inhabitants for more than a hundred years until James Cook arrived in 1769 on the first of his three voyages. Cook traveled around and charted both the North and the South Islands, and was amazingly accurate considering the navigation problems of the time. He returned in 1773 and again in 1777, recounting in his journals his view that New Zealand was a land of promise, where settlers could build a

comfortable life. Early European traders, though, were more interested in making quick money than in settling. The profits to be gained from whaling, sealing, and natural resources such as timber and flax were enough to have them returning to Europe on a continual basis to sell their gains and reap the rewards. New Zealand's coasts had attracted mostly British and Australian whalers until the American captain Eber Bunker sailed into Northland's Doubtless Bay in the late 1700s. In 1847 the world's whaling fleet comprised nine hundred ships, of which just over seven hundred belonged to the USA. When a ban on the Americans, excluding them from Australian ports, was lifted, New Zealand became the attraction, especially as provisions were cheap, with no duties or restrictions. No wonder the first American millionaires were whale-ship owners and not oil moguls! Russell, or Kororareka, as it was called then, was home to the whaling fraternity, and was known not so much as the refuge for carousing whalers as the "refuse," if Darwin's observations are to be believed. So wild was the town, with its reputation as the "hell-hole of the Pacific," that it made itself a natural target for missionaries. It was also where the rebel chief Hone Heke, who had been the first Maori leader to sign the Treaty of Waitangi, had became disillusioned with British government and felled that symbol of English authority, the flagpole, four times.

War . . .

At first, the country had been administered from New South Wales, the region from which Britain colonized this part of the world. While governors were appointed to carry out the orders and uphold the laws of the British government, in effect they were in charge because they were on the spot. There had been some French interest in New Zealand, mainly in support for the head of the Catholic mission, Bishop Pompallier. Plans were made by France to establish a settlement at Akaroa in the South Island but, by the time the French settlers arrived the country was firmly in British hands. The myth still persists that there was a race by the two powers to get there first, with Captain Stanley in HMS *Britomart* being dispatched from the Bay of Islands to establish sovereignty; the French, for once, did not contest this, but to this day Akaroa has a French flavor.

New Zealand's most renowned governor was Captain (later Sir) George

Grey, who did his best to uphold the spirit of equality contained in the Treaty of Waitangi. However, relations between Maori and Pakeha (the Maori word for "white men") deteriorated, with Maori concerned at the effect the settlers were having on their society, and the Pakeha showing little regard for Maori rights. Even though a constitution had been drawn up by the British government in 1846, Grey considered the country too unsettled for this to be implemented. Many settlers called him "the great dictator," even though he was the main author of the constitution of 1852, which granted white men (but not women) the vote. In 1854, the settlers had their own parliament, and two years later a greater degree of autonomy. There were elected assemblies in each province of the country as well as a General Assembly in Auckland. New Zealand was now self-governing in all domestic matters except "native policy." The situation between the Maori and the British continued to deteriorate, however, mainly because of

disagreements over land and, by 1860, it had escalated into full-scale warfare. The Maori called these wars *to riri Pakeha* ("the white man's anger, or quarrel"), while the British called them the Maori Wars, and they continued until 1872.

. . . and Peace

By the late 1800s the situation had calmed. Over 100,000 immigrants arrived in the 1870s, including families with children. Most came from Britain, and it has always been a source of pride to Kiwis, and a point of differentiation from Australia, that their country was never a penal settlement and their heritage not of the convict variety. New Zealand developed a small-farm economy with wide-scale sheep farming, and gradually became self-reliant. In the 1880s the worldwide depression impacted on the country, resulting in low prices for wool, its main export. Although the discovery of gold in the South Island brought prosperity to this area, economic problems needed to be addressed and the emergence of political parties at this time led to the Liberal Party's taking office for the next twenty years (1891–1912) and passing a series of laws aimed at improving the quality of life. The government purchased large tracts of land to assist families to farm, factory conditions improved, trade unions were encouraged, social security was implemented, and women's lives changed for the better, New Zealand priding itself on the fact that it was the first country to grant women the right to vote, in 1893.

By the turn of the century New Zealand had become much more settled. A countrywide rail network was built, and on the communications side the telegraph, telephone, and penny postage were introduced. The workforce had become more organized, and professional groups such as doctors, teachers, and accountants formed national associations to protect their interests, as did employers, trade unions, and farmers. The land, no longer pioneer territory, had become more tamed and cultivated. Sports, too, had become more organized, with the New Zealand Rugby Football Union established in 1892. New Zealanders had begun to develop a sense of nationhood and decided not to join the Australian federation of 1901. In 1907 New Zealand gained Dominion status within the British Empire.

The Emergence of a Nation

Ties with Britain remained strong, and it was loyalty that led to New Zealand's sending troops—the first colony to do so—to South Africa in 1899 to fight for Britain in the Boer War. Again in the First World War New Zealand quickly rallied to the mother country's side. This was its first major foray into the international arena, and marked its emergence as a separate nation rather than "merely Englishmen living abroad." Thousands of New Zealanders died on various battle fronts, and the disastrous landing at Gallipoli in 1915 by the Anzacs, the joint Australian and New Zealand Army Corps, marked New Zealand's coming of age as a nation.

By 1886 more than half of New Zealand's European population of 578,500 had been born

GALLIPOLI

The Gallipoli Campaign was one of the great disasters of the First World War. The Allied strategy, brainchild of Winston Churchill, was to end the war early, creating a new war front by forcing a way through the Dardanelles and linking up with Russia. Turkey was allied to Germany, and the heavily fortified Gallipoli peninsula dominated the Dardanelles, the straits connecting the Mediterranean to the Black Sea After failing to take out the Turkish batteries by bombardment from the sea, it was decided to launch full-scale landings. A combined force of Anzacs, the British 29th Division, and French colonial troops landed on the Turkish peninsula on April 25, 1915. The coast was precipitous, with few good landing places, and the combination of superior Turkish firepower and poor Allied generalship resulted in a bloody withdrawal in which 2,700 New Zealanders died and another 4,700 were wounded. The date has been kept as a day of national mourning in both New Zealand and Australia.

there, and people often identified themselves regionally, as an "Aucklander," an "Otagan," or a "Wellingtonian." Since large-scale settlement days, regional differences had been (and still are) marked, and regional rivalry has been a healthy feature of New Zealand life. Social differences between the six provinces were really due to the different methods of settlement. The town of Christchurch was more English, Dunedin more Scottish, and Auckland more Australian, although today Auckland is considered more American. There was also a distinction between the four country provinces of Wellington, Nelson, Canterbury, and Otago, and those of Auckland and Taranaki, where small mixed farming was more common.

However, there were major differences between the North and South Islands. As a consequence of the gold rushes of the 1870s the South Island's population remained larger until 1896. Most Maori lived in the temperate North, and this was where Maori and Pakeha contested control of the land. In the South Island pastoral settlement and the gold rushes were less contested.

New Zealand's standard of living compared well to the rest of the world, and the implementation of social welfare measures, such as old-age pensions, which were introduced in 1898, maternity hospitals, and in 1911, under Dick Seddon's government, widows' pensions, commanded international respect. The general election of 1911 ended Liberal dominance and gave way to the new Reform Party, led by "Farmer Bill" Massey, who upheld hard work, supported the farmers, and respected the British Empire. He encouraged the adoption of the New Zealand flag in 1901, which led to flag-raising ceremonies in schools, and to children singing patriotic songs and speaking their own sort of English, with a colonial twang that later grew into the Kiwi accent.

After a few prosperous years following the First World War, the 1920s were a time of hardship in the country, and the worldwide Great Depression severely impacted on New Zealand. Export prices for primary produce fell and the plight of the farmers, many burdened with heavy mortgages, was felt throughout the country. Unemployment in the towns and general discontent led to riots. A conservative coalition government failed to remedy the situation and a new Labour Party under Micky Savage, which took power in 1935, managed to revive an already recovering economy with solutions that concentrated on improving conditions for the average family. The Welfare State was extended with the Social Security Act of 1938. A state housing program was begun, public works spending increased, and a health care system was set up.

The Second World War again saw New Zealand troops supporting Great Britain, fighting alongside fellow democracies to save the world from Nazi Germany. The fall of Singapore to the Japanese signaled a change in attitude in the country as New Zealanders recognized that Britain could no longer be relied upon to guarantee their security.

The 1931 Statute of Westminster had affirmed equality of status between Britain and the dominions and effectively granted independence to New Zealand, which in 1935 became totally responsible for its own foreign affairs. However, independence was formally proclaimed only in 1947, when the Statute was adopted by the New Zealand parliament.

As the USA had protected both Australia and New Zealand from Japan during the Second World War, New Zealand felt obliged to support it. Thus in the 1950s it sent armed forces to Korea, to help the Americans in their fight against Communism. However, when troops were sent to support America in Vietnam, for the first time the New Zealand public voiced its opposition. There were fears that the conflict could escalate into a major nuclear war, and also the feeling that the Vietnamese should decide their own form of government. Later, this antinuclear stance would bring the country into conflict with both the USA and France, whose nuclear tests in the Pacific led to the French Secret Services taking action against Greenpeace's *Rainbow Warrior*, which was blown up as it lay at anchor in Auckland's harbor on July 10, 1985.

Postwar

The 1950s saw growing prosperity in New Zealand. The economy stabilized under the more conservative National Party, many new industries such as the steel industry started, and the country became more industrialized. In later years more of the Maori population moved to cities and, with more women going out to work, the "Women's Lib" movement flourished. Changes in the law ensured equal opportunity for everyone, from job accessibility to housing and education, whatever the person's sex, race, ethnic origin, marital status, or religious beliefs. Other groups of workers came not only from Britain and Europe but also from the Pacific Islands—Fiji,

Tonga, the Cook Islands, and Western Samoa. The effects of the oil crises of the 1970s and the worldwide recession in the 1980s were felt in New Zealand, but probably the most significant occurrence in modern times was Britain's joining the European Economic Community in 1973, which had not only an economic effect on the country but also a profound psychological impact. The apron strings were finally cut! In 1986, the Constitution Act ended Britain's residual legislative powers, and New Zealand became solely responsible for its own government (which it had been, in effect, for years). It remains, however, a key member of the British Commonwealth.

The Labour Party retook power in 1984, but the National Party returned in 1990, largely continuing with Labour's free-market policies, which had revolutionized the economy. The National government, which held power until 1999, diminished the power of trade unions and opened up the labor market. The change to proportional representation in 1996 meant that future governments by either Labour or National have had to take into account smaller parties and frequently enter into coalitions with them.

Modern Times

New Zealand today is much more integrated in the world, and is probably more influenced by America, having shaken off its British past. The subsequent political, economic, and social changes, particularly with regard to its many immigrants, mean that it is no longer a colonial outpost of Britain but a multicultural Pacific nation. Nevertheless, unlike Australia, where there is an active republican sentiment, New Zealanders have not expressed any fervent desire to cast aside the monarchy. In 1994 the then Prime Minister, Jim Bolger, initiated the debate on New Zealand becoming a republic. He argued for greater focus and union with the Asia-Pacific region. A poll taken in 2010, before a visit from British Prince William, found that only 29.4 percent of respondents preferred to see New Zealand become a republic.

New Zealand still opposes the testing and use of nuclear weapons and takes a prominent part in UN peacekeeping activities throughout the world. It has close relations with Australia at government level, the respective prime ministers and cabinet ministers holding annual formal talks on issues such as health, education, and quarantine, among many others. The two countries cooperate closely internationally and regionally, specifically in the Pacific Islands Forum, and are currently involved in the Cairns Group, a coalition of seventeen agricultural exporting countries, which are seeking freedom of trade in agriculture. A treaty signed in 2004 by both countries defined maritime boundaries in the Tasman Sea and areas of the southwestern Pacific Ocean.

New Zealand shared an alliance with Australia and the USA (ANZUS) from the end of Second World War until the mid-1980s. With Australia it established the Closer Defence Relations (CDR), which although not a formal treaty, brings together a large number of agreements on policy, intelligence and security, logistics, and science and technology. There is significant operational collaboration between the two defense forces: recent years shared engagements include operations in Timor Leste, Bougainville, Solomon Islands, and Tonga. Forces from both countries amalgamated in operations in East Timor during the humanitarian crisis of 1999–2002 and in the Solomon Islands during the civil unrest and subsequent coup of 2000, forming a South Pacific security force.

THE ECONOMY

New Zealand is a resourceful nation, largely due to its many and diverse immigrants, who arrived with little and had to look to the land to sustain them. The perception that it is a country of sheep and dairy farmers, where sheep outnumber the people, is not wholly inaccurate, but this does not reflect the present reality. For one thing, although there are indeed still more sheep than people, numbers are dwindling—there being today twelve sheep for every New Zealander where previously there were twenty. Farming is still the backbone of the economy, but traditional earners, which formed 90 percent of exports in the 1960s, have been joined by newer industries such as tourism, wine production, and filmmaking.

Britain's entry into the EEC, at a time when 91 percent of New Zealand's butter and 65 percent of its meat (mostly lamb) were exported directly to the UK, forced farmers to find new markets and products. The kiwi fruit was one of these, and New Zealand's own breed of sheep, the Corriedale, another, the latter providing both

high-quality wool and good meat. The Corriedale has become the second-most important breed in the world, after the Merino. New Zealand's largest export market today is China followed by Australia, the USA, Japan, and Korea, with the UK only in sixth place. move pic to other side ofpage.

Rogernomics

Farming has become more skilled—rather than being replaced by the financial sector, particularly with the attempts of the country to become the finance center of the South Pacific in the 1980s, or by tourism, which although significant has not boomed as much as anticipated. Much of the change can be attributed to Roger Douglas, Labour's finance minister in 1984. He decided that farming should not be treated as a revered institution, resting on its laurels and entitled to state protection, but should become a business like any other. Douglas instituted a program of deregulation, privatization, and downsizing. With the elimination of subsidies farmers became more focused on marketing. He reduced tariffs, removed quotas, lifted controls on prices, wages, and foreign exchange, and deregulated the labor market. As a tribute to its instigator, this free-market approach, the likes of which had not been seen before in the modern, Western world, was labeled "Rogernomics." It was seen as so beneficial that, when Labour was voted out of office in 1991, Douglas's counterpart in the National Party, Ruth Richardson, continued the policy.

"Rogernomics" has undoubtedly contributed to New Zealand's place among the world's richer economies, albeit at the lower end of middle-rich countries, according to the Organization for Economic Cooperation and Development, whose gauge is material output rather than standard of living. Even so New Zealand, which has about 0.1 percent of the world's population, produces 0.3 percent of the world's material output.

Resources and Products
New Zealand also has its own natural resources. Gold and some silver are still produced in east Otago and in the Coromandel Peninsula, while alluvial mining occurs in the West Coast region. Iron is found on the North Island's west coast and mined at Waikato for use in a local steel mill and further south for export. Its offshore resources include iron sands,

seafloor gold and base metals, phosphate and other minerals. Oil and gas (petroleum) are important to the New Zealand economy. Oil is a major export earner for the country, and gas is used by the domestic economy. New Zealand aims to become an attractive global destination for petroleum exploration and production investment. It can also exploit its geothermal energy. Today 40 percent of New Zealand's primary energy is supplied by renewable energy sources.

Forestry is another resource, and products such as timber, pulp, and paper account for 3 percent of New Zealand's GDP and is estimated to be worth NZ$3.5bn. The seafood industry sustainably harvests about 600,000 tonnes from wild fisheries and aquaculture each year. The value of this harvest ranges from $1.2 to $1.5 billion per annum. Seafood exports consistently rank as New Zealand's fourth or fifth largest export earner. Fish, including rock lobster, tuna, mussels, and hoki, and fish products, account for 4 percent of all exports.

Manufacturing accounts for just under 20 percent of New Zealand's GDP—mainly food and beverages, followed by machinery and equipment. More sophisticated industrial design, new technology, and research have led to considerable worldwide success for everyday products such as domestic appliances , furniture, and buses.

Geographical influences have led to New Zealand's status as a world leader both in earthquake-resistant structures and in yacht design. It is also making a mark in the field of biotechnology. New Zealand has captured a share of the world's largest industry— tourism—taking advantage of the America's Cup yachting competition and the success of the locally made *Lord of the Rings* film trilogy, the third of which, *The Return of the King*, won eleven Oscars at the 2004 Academy Awards, and has helped boost the New Zealand film industry.

GOVERNMENT AND POLITICS

New Zealand is a parliamentary democracy in the Westminster tradition, with a constitutional monarchy. On her accession in 1952, Queen Elizabeth II was proclaimed "Queen of this realm and all her other realms," and she reigns over New Zealand independently of her position as Queen of the United Kingdom. The prime minister is the head of government and must have the confidence of the House of Representatives to govern. The House is presided over by the Speaker, who is elected by the House's 120 members. There is no upper house

of parliament—the Legislative Council, as it was called, was abolished in 1950. While the House of Representatives proposes and passes the laws of the land, as well as approving the raising and spending of money by government, all bills need the assent of the Queen, or her representative, to become law although, as in the UK, this assent is not traditionally withheld. A government's term of office is three years, and while it is compulsory to enroll to vote, it is not compulsory to vote. The seat of government has been in Wellington since 1865. Prior to that it was in Auckland from 1840 and previously in the Bay of Islands.

In New Zealand, the Queen's representative is the Governor General, who is head of state. It is his or her duty to summon, prorogue, or dissolve parliament. Dame Patsy Reddy, appointed in 2016, is the current Governor-General. The post also carries the position of titular commander-in-chief of the armed forces.

Although this highest office in the land used to be filled by Britain's minor aristocracy, it has for many years been held by New Zealand citizens, appointed by the Queen on the prime minister's recommendation. The role, as is the Queen's, is symbolic and ceremonial. It is interesting that New Zealand does not have a written constitution or Bill of Rights. Acts of parliament direct how the country is governed, and certain customary rules are upheld, although these do not have any legal standing. Acts of parliament safeguard specific rights, such as the Bill of Rights Act of 1990, which specifies the rights of citizens when dealing with government, and the Human Rights Act of 1993, which prohibits discrimination on various grounds.

The Voting System
A major change in the electoral system was instituted in 1993, when FPP (First Past the Post, where candidates obtaining the majority in a constituency were returned to parliament) was replaced by MMP (Mixed Member Proportional, which is modeled on the German system). Now, of the 120 seats in parliament, seventy-one members are elected by popular vote in single member constituencies, including seven Maori constituencies, and fifty proportional seats are chosen from party lists, all to serve three-year terms. Voters therefore have two votes, one for an individual local MP, and the second for a political party. Each party will have drawn up a list of parliamentary candidates, in order of priority. In the second vote, the more votes a party secures the more members of parliament it will have. If the number of its individual local MPs is lower

than the total number of party votes it receives, its parliamentary total is made up from the party list.

Maoris have had separate representation in parliament since 1867, and Maori voters may choose to be on either the general electoral roll or the Maori electoral roll, which was instituted in 1975. The number of seats in parliament may change according to the number of voters who elect to be on the Maori electoral roll.

The main advantage of the change to proportional representation is that minor parties have a greater opportunity to enter parliament, but the downside is that coalition and minority government are more likely, with all the attendant problems this can bring. It is a frequent subject of discussion with New Zealanders, who often feel that a party will put more effort into accommodating its coalition partner over issues upon which they may differ just to stay in power, rather than finding solutions to problems that need addressing. All citizens and permanent residents of New Zealand over the age of eighteen years are eligible to vote, but only New Zealand citizens are entitled to sit in parliament.

The Legal System

New Zealand's judiciary, which interprets and enforces the law, is separate from parliament, which enacts the laws, and the executive, which runs the daily affairs of government. Judges are appointed by the Governor General. There is a hierarchy of courts in the country—district courts, the High Court, the Court of Appeal, and the Supreme Court, which is the final court of appeal in the land. It was only in 2003 that the right of appeal to the British Privy Council from New Zealand courts was abolished. Courts operate on the trial by jury system, inherited from the UK, while judges act as neutral referees to the defense and prosecution. There are also special courts such as the Family Court and the Youth Court, both of which operate under the district courts sector; the Employment Court, which hears cases relating to the Employment Relations Act; and the Environment Court, which hears matters relating to the Resource Management Act. A Maori Land Court, established in 1865 as the Native Land Court of New Zealand, deals with issues relating to land held on tenures peculiar to the Maori.

Political Parties

The National Party and the Labour Party are currently New Zealand's two main parties although, when political parties first emerged in the 1890s, it was the Liberal Party that came to power. It is historically regarded as the first real political party. By 1916, two other parties had emerged: Reform in 1909 and Labour in 1916. The Reform Party was created during the Liberal Party's long period of control (1891–1911) by more conservative Liberals who broke away. The growth of the Labour Party at this time resulted in Liberal and Reform joining together to oppose it and thus the National Party was formed. A plethora of parties have formed since then, notably the Alliance, New Zealand, and Green, all of which now have a greater say in parliament under the MMP system.

The party currently holding office is the National Party; it is characterized as a center-right party and is led by John Key. Following the September 2014 general election, it governs in coalition with United Future, ACT, and the Maori Party. The official opposition party is Labour, headed by Andrew Little, former national secretary of New Zealand's largest trade union EPMU.

Political parties can be registered or unregistered, the former being permitted to submit a party list and so able to receive votes in the MMP electoral system. Unregistered parties are permitted to nominate candidates for individual electorates. Besides those mentioned the current parliament also has members from the New Zealand First and Green parties.

There are eighteen registered parties, which include some rather interesting titles: the Internet Party, the Bill and Ben Party, and the Legalise Cannabis Party!

A further half-dozen unregistered parties can be added to the foregoing, which means that Kiwis are certainly spoiled for choice if not understandably confused.

MAJOR CITIES AND SOME AREAS OF INTEREST

New Zealand's capital is Wellington, the seat of government. The Cabinet Offices are housed in a building called the "Beehive," because of the spherical shape of its extension. Wellington is subject to somewhat inclement weather, particularly wind, but is a city of good ethnic restaurants, culture, and the

arts—the Te Papa museum houses many treasures.
Wellington was home to the writer Katherine
Mansfield, and the colonial buildings of Thorndon,
where she grew up, are worth visiting, as the area
captures the charm of the significant migratory time
of the 1860s and '70s.

The North Island

The attractions of Auckland, known as the "City of
Sails," and home to one-third of the population, are
of a maritime nature, centered on its waterfront.
The Waitemata Harbor and the Hauraki Gulf are
where sailors spend their leisure time and where the
America's Cup was held. The Kelly Tarlton's Antarctic
Encounter and Underwater World, just out of the
center of town, is popular with tourists.

The Bay of Islands and Northland are the seat
of New Zealand's history, as this was where Maori
and Pakeha first made contact, where the Treaty

of Waitangi was signed, and where the carousing whalers enjoyed their time in the erstwhile capital of Russell. A boat trip (one such is called the Cream Run, and dates back to the time when milk was delivered) around the Bay of Islands is a must—there are approximately 150 islands scattered along the coastline. This is also game-fishing area, and a favorite haunt of the American writer Zane Grey. The extensive kauri forests on the west coast around Waipoua are also worth a stop. No visit to New Zealand is complete without a trip to Rotorua, an area of thermal activity where erupting geysers, bubbling mud pools, and the smell of sulfur abound. It is straight out of the dinosaur age.

The South Island

Fiordland is noted for the amazing beauty of its lakes and mountains. Queenstown, the premier resort in South Island, offering fantastic skiing in winter and in the summer months. There are plenty of hikes, such as the Milford Track, Queen Charlotte Track, and Abel Tasman, to be enjoyed by walkers and, of course, New Zealand's highest mountain, Mount Cook. Omarama is an internationally renowned gliding destination. As Dunedin is known for its Scottish heritage, and is the coldest of the main centers, so Christchurch, the third largest town, has an English feel. South Canterbury was home to Richard Pearse, who built a powered flying machine and in 1902 and 1903, perhaps just before the Wright brothers, made some early successful flights; and also to the author Ngaio Marsh.

Stewart Island, roughly 19 miles (30 km) south of South Island, is the destination for birdwatching enthusiasts. It is home to the southern brown kiwi (Tokoeka), Blue penguin, and the rare Yellow-eyed penguin. Eighty-five percent of the island is national park, and with174 miles (280 km) of walking tracks, the island is a hikers' paradise. Because of its very southerly position it is advisable to visit in summer.

VALUES & ATTITUDES

NATIONAL PRIDE

New Zealanders came from an assortment of nationalities and backgrounds, but over time they

gained a sense of identity, which has grown into the "Kiwi" persona. The Kiwi is the national bird of New Zealand, and the word "Kiwi" has become synonymous with "New Zealander." Kiwis call New Zealand "Godzone," from "God's own country," which is attributed to Dick Seddon, New Zealand's prime minister in the 1890s.

On its journey to nationhood, New Zealand chose not to join the Federation of Australia, which was established in 1901, and become its seventh state. In 1948 a separate citizenship was created and the practice of calling Britain "home" more or less died out in the 1950s. Britain's national anthem, in use since 1840, has now been ousted by "God Defend New Zealand," with Maori verses sung before the English, which in 1977 was given equal status with the British anthem. In 1977 the words "British subject" were removed from the New Zealand passport.

Two national holidays every year have a distinctly nationalistic tone—Waitangi Day on February 6, which celebrates the signing of the Treaty, was declared a holiday in 1974 and Anzac Day on April 25, which commemorates the landing of New Zealand and Australian troops at Gallipoli in the First World War. New Zealanders will be impressed if visitors are aware of these two events.

New Zealand used the British coat of arms until 1911 after it became a self-governing Dominion in 1907.

There is no official national flower, but the silver fern appears on all national sports clothing and army insignia, and has become an unofficial emblem. The red *pohutukawa* and yellow *kowhai* flowers are also symbolic of New Zealand's summer and spring respectively. As for the word "Kiwi," it has never received official sanction—perhaps because it is a bird that cannot fly. During the First World War New Zealanders were nicknamed "Tommy Fernleaf," which may have been a reason for the adoption of the shorter term!

The New Zealand flag, which was based on the British Blue Ensign design of 1869, was adopted in 1902 but was officially declared the national flag as late as 1981. The four five-pointed red stars represent the southern constellation (minus its faintest star),

although some consider that they were intended to signify the four countries of the United Kingdom. Australia, in contrast, has white stars loosely scattered on its flag, and it is a good idea not to confuse the two!

There had been numerous calls to replace the flag with a design more representative of the New Zealand nation. The debate, which had been going on since the 1970s, was finally settled at the Second Flag referendum held in March 2016. The process was a long and costly one. The Flag Consideration Panel judged 10,292 flag designs and shortlisted forty designs, which was whittled down to five alternatives that were put

forward to be ranked in the first referendum, held in 2015. The Silver Fern Flag, designed by Kyle Lockwood, was chosen to stand against the old British Blue Ensign design. With the question "which flag do you think best represents the shared values and beliefs and how we see ourselves now and into the future" New Zealanders chose to go with the status quo.

This keenness to be a "Kiwi" is part and parcel of an enthusiastic patriotism, which emphasizes the fact, and maybe acts as a reminder, that they are one nation, albeit a new one. This may account for the Kiwis sometimes going "over the top," as in giving their winning America's Cup team of 2000 a tickertape parade down Auckland's Queen Street and only a year later castigating one of that team, Russell Coutts, for his decision to leave Team NZ and join a Swiss team because it was a more lucrative prospect. He won the America's Cup for Switzerland in 1993 and was, sadly, branded a traitor in certain circles.

You will go a long way with New Zealanders if you start by complimenting them on their country, and that is not hard to do, as it is a place of great natural beauty and charm. They are also eager to be seen to be part of the world, as for so long they have been on the edge. Consequently, it is not uncommon to see various towns displaying signs saying, "Home of the world's biggest brown trout," " . . . largest fish and chip shop," or " . . . best ice cream." You may see many signs making the same claims! New Zealanders are also proud of their "hokey-pokey" ice cream, a sort of butterscotch offering, which they consider their unique invention. Shops and businesses also get in on the act and take it a step further by using the prefix "Kiwi," whether to describe food, sports, or more technical activities. Further, if "nz" can somehow be incorporated into a word then it must be done. New Zealanders, therefore, are EnZers, and many businesses demonstrate their patriotism by adapting their spellings accordingly. Companies are called Fernz, Newztel, Kidz First, and Kay-Zed Cruises, and there is even Split Enz, a rock group.

It is no wonder that, according to *NZ Insider*, a newsletter for those immigrating or relocating to New Zealand, in the controversial National Certificate of Education (NCEA) examinations, the school-leaving qualification introduced in 2002, nearly 40 percent of students failed their English essay papers because of poor spelling and grammar!

The same nationalistic theme can be seen in car license plates, although the more obscure and elliptical these are, the better—there's nothing as unimaginative as a simple "007" here, or even just your initials. For instance, "BERNZ 1" shows not only that it belongs to Bernie, but also that she's a real Kiwi patriot. Then you get plates such as "THE01" (the naughty one); "XCAV8R" (excavator—Kiwis love to dig), and even GR8TVET" (to whom you take your pet, if you like the less modest type), and "GGRRR" (which may indicate the ferocity of the occupant). More obtuse thinking is revealed with 2ND TOO, which does not mean "second as well," after all, who wants to be second? Rather it means "second to none." Personalized license plates are big business in this country, and plates change hands for thousands of dollars.

ON BEING EQUAL AND PC

Like Australia, New Zealand prides itself on being an egalitarian society that has grown from its historical roots or, rather, its lack of them. Inequality was an old-world theme, and equality is the new, especially in the United States and Australia, which influenced

New Zealand's development. However, whether they are the "Yankees of the South Pacific," as the American historian Frank Parsons considered, is another matter. Interestingly, though, the first arrivals in the 1840s were not from either the highest or the lowest classes but rather from the upper working or lower middle classes. They were dubbed "the anxious classes" by William Wakefield, the principal agent of the New Zealand Company (formed to sell land to settlers, many of whom bought sight unseen in London). It was fear of poverty rather than persecution or starvation that drove the first immigrants to the new country. The intention was to create a classless society. The laborers wanted to be as well off as "the nobs back home," but the nobs, who did come to New Zealand thought it "rather dull and unkempt."

The early pioneers had to be prepared to work, and the work was certainly not for weaklings, or "lighties." Forests had to be cleared—thick bush and swamps were often all that could be seen on landing, timber workers felled trees with axes and vast crosscut saws measuring twice their own height—and miners

worked long hours panning gold in the harsh Otago climate. The experience of these early days contributed to the present Kiwi attitude of "mucking in" and "not getting above oneself," with everyone being treated the same. Everyone is on a first-name basis. The plumber will arrive and say something like "Well, John (or Ann), what's the problem?" It is not a case of being familiar, but of not standing on ceremony. The New Zealanders are naturally friendly and helpful and, even more to the point, have time. Ask them a question and the answer will be carefully considered. They are patient, too, and will clarify at length should the answer not be understood.

Probably allied with this is the attitude of being "PC," or politically correct. This has probably arisen because, in a nation of immigrants, Kiwis have learned to be aware of different backgrounds, to treat others as equals, and to avoid making tactless comments. They tread carefully, and hate to offend. Statements by others that they perceive to be anything less than PC are usually countered by such comments as, "Yeah, but you might also consider . . ." or, simply, "I reckon," which does not actually say anything. This has the result of making them appear noncommittal, and it may not be easy to establish where they stand on certain issues until you know them better. You are not expected to give your life history on meeting. In fact, the Kiwi lack of inquiry or interest in this department can be somewhat disquieting, but it is all part of not wanting to appear rude or inquisitive. It is not that important to him anyway. He certainly does not want to hear from you how successful, rich, or whatever else you might be. He would rather learn your history gradually, and not have it "in his face." It is all very low-key, and if you want to fit in, that is how you should be, too. The Kiwi might, for instance, respond to a comment such as, "We've just got back from a wonderful holiday in outer Mongolia" with, "Oh yeah—nice. Did you manage to see the All Blacks match against Australia?" which reveals his priorities.

The "tall poppy" syndrome of cutting people down to size still exists in New Zealand, and success or achievement is not readily recognized without some feeling that such achievers may be getting "above themselves." The feeling is that neither wealth nor prestige should carry any prerogative, and woe to those who think it does. New Zealanders are, by and large, happy with their lot, do not have great aspirations, and are not always understanding of those who do.

There is no doubt, however, that the trappings of capitalism are appearing in a much more noticeable way than before. In Auckland in particular money talks, and there are more grand, architect-designed houses, flashy cars, and prestigious residential areas, such as Paritai Drive.

RELIGION

The Church of England and the Free Church of Scotland both settled immigrants in the nineteenth century, despite Hongi Hika's statement that Christianity was no good as a religion for warriors! He was the Ngapuhi chief who, in 1820, was presented to the court of King George IV and showered with presents. He promptly sold these on his return to New Zealand for muskets, which he used to great effect against his enemies. The prominence of churches throughout New Zealand shows that Christianity is still very much part of the life of the country, although congregations have fallen, following the world trend, and the Church's influence has declined.

The 2013 censuses shows that over half of all New Zealanders are Christian, with Catholicism now the largest denomination, having recently overtaken the position from the Anglican Church. The Presbyterians follow closely behind in numbers with a host of other Non-conformist Protestant denominations. The variety of immigrants has meant that Islam, Hinduism, and Buddhism have grown, although each has only around 50,000 followers. Jews have been in the country since the nineteenth century, and there are synagogues in most cities and major towns.

The Maori have two indigenous religions, which are mostly Christian-based. Ringatu was founded by a Maori prophet, and dates back to the nineteenth century, and the larger, Ratana, was founded by a faith healer in the twentieth century. Within several established Christian denominations, the Maori have also introduced some of their own features into the liturgy. Thus you may get the Lord's Prayer said in both English and Maori, or half and half, or there will be a separate Maori service.

HUMOR

New Zealanders are not known for a rollicking sense of humor. They are quiet and understated, and this ties in with their generally restrained behavior and, some would say, parochial attitudes. Jokes are often made about Australia and sheep, although jibes about the former are often the same jokes heard about New Zealanders told by Australians. The many jokes about sheep have arisen due to their proliferation over people. Some sheep jokes (or, as they have been termed, "ewe-phemisms") contain puns on song titles, such as, "I'll never find another you/ewe." The Kiwis particularly favored this song, as it was an Australian group that sang it.

Differences in accent between the two countries make for further opportunities. As the off-color NZ joke goes, a farmer, with an Aussie accent of course, who has been caught having unnatural relations with a sheep, is asked if he should rather be shearing it. His reply is "I'm not shearing (pronounced 'sharing') this sheep with anyone." It is ironic that one of New Zealand's best-known comedians, John Clarke, known in his typical persona of Fred Dagg, the epitome of an early farmer dressed in black undershirt and gum boots, has spent more time playing to audiences in Australia than in his own country.

Australians are frequently the subject of Kiwi humor (and vice versa), and diplomacy, seemingly, is not an issue. During the 1980s, the then Prime Minister of New Zealand Rob Muldoon was asked to explain why so many New Zealanders were leaving the country to work in Australia. His comment was that by doing so, they were raising the average IQ of both countries.

New Zealand's remoteness has been another area of mirth, even with Kiwis, who can poke fun at themselves. There are many variations of the well-worn instruction, attributed to a Qantas air hostess, "We will be landing shortly in New Zealand. Please put your watches forward two hours . . . and back twenty years." Kiwis' recognition of their still not being quite "in the world" is typified by the announcement that the New Zealand Space Agency is temporarily closed due to a lack of beer and pies!

Among Kiwis, the New Zealand accent is another target of jokes, particularly with regard to its rising inflection, which varies throughout the country and makes every sentence sound like a question. Further opportunities in this vein are the rolled "r" sound as pronounced by the inhabitants of the southernmost part of the South Island and the "eh," which Maori and North Islanders add to the end of sentences. This appears to have originated from "*ne*?" which is often used at the end of Maori sentences, and means "isn't it?"

ATTITUDES TOWARD OTHERS

New Zealanders are, by and large, a friendly nation, despite a natural reserve. Thus, social progress can be slow, and the same is expected from you, so it is as well not be too forward or too friendly. However, due to their down-to-earth, egalitarian attitude, they are very informal, disliking titles. Because of this they appear to treat everyone equally, and pulling rank will not have the desired effect, and probably even the opposite one. New Zealanders are patient—everyone must wait his turn but, should you attempt to butt in line, even with a harmless question, you will be told very politely that you will be dealt with when, and only when, your time comes. They are very much followers of fair play. Their tolerance and patience is not a characteristic often seen in the faster-track, first-world countries. Similarly, their old-world attitudes mean that they are naturally trusting of others until there is a reason not to be.

ATTITUDES TOWARD WOMEN

Women are very well represented in the country's top jobs, including that of prime minister. Historically, women played a vitally important role in society. When the early settlers were trying to make a living on the land, the women had more scope and responsibility than they'd had in England. They brought up and educated the children, as schools were too far away and usually expensive; they took care of the sick, and earned cash from the sale of their produce such as butter and dairy foods, but probably their most important role was to moderate the drinking of the male pioneers to soften their coarse manners. It is not, therefore, surprising that the legacy of these women in society today is considerable, and that in many areas they have challenged their menfolk.

New Zealand has a progressive attitude to women: it was the first country to allow all adult women to vote. After two decades of campaigning on a platform for an equal society, the 1893 Women's

Suffrage Petition was presented to and passed through Parliament, twenty-five years before women gained the vote in the UK. In that same year Elizabeth Yates also became Mayor of Onehunga, the first time such a post had been held by a female anywhere in the British Empire.

Yet despite this glowing history the gender pay gap in New Zealand persists and in 2015 this stood at 11.8 percent.

ATTITUDES TOWARD MAORIS

Although Maori are still disadvantaged in New Zealand, their plight has never been as serious as that of the Australian Aborigines. Many Pakeha New Zealanders consider that the land claim issue has gone on for long enough, and that some sort of deadline needs to be set. However, when the baby of a prominent Land Claims lawyer, herself of Maori descent, was kidnapped and held for ransom, the nation united as one and people tuned in to the radio and TV throughout the ordeal, all expressing their concern at the crime. Never mind that the mother was wealthy as a result of her work for Maori in a controversial field; this was definitely not fair play in anyone's book. Many New Zealanders are also concerned about the divisions that are arising because of privileges and even "handouts" that are granted to Maori rather than Pakeha, which has led to a "them" and "us" attitude. "We are all New Zealanders!" is the cry, with an underlying belief that all should be treated equally. It is interesting that the parliamentarian Winston Peters, who is of Maori descent, fought the

last general election on a platform of "one people, one law for all and one electoral roll," as there is a separate Maori electoral roll, the only qualification being self-identification. Probably even more to the point in New Zealand is that there is a Maori only rugby team, the Maori All Blacks.

Similarly, the government's policy of allowing so many Asians into the country has been questioned by New Zealanders who feel "overrun," and this group has become a target for the some of the more disgruntled elements of society.

chapter three

CUSTOMS & TRADITIONS

PUBLIC HOLIDAYS

By and large, public holidays are seen as days off work or an excuse for a long weekend. However, Anzac Day is treated with reverence, with old and young attending sunrise services throughout the country. Services outside the Auckland Museum attract crowds of thousands, as do similar services in the other major cities of Wellington and Christchurch.

Similarly respected is Waitangi Day. It is a day to reflect on the 1840 Treaty, New Zealand's founding

January 1	New Year's Day
January 2	New Year's Observance
February 6	Waitangi Day
March/April	Good Friday, Easter Saturday, Easter Monday
April 25	Anzac Day
First Monday in June	The Queen's Birthday
Fourth Monday in October	Labour Day
December 25	Christmas Day
December 26	Boxing Day

document and is celebrated mainly by the Maori. It has often been the focus of protest by Maori activists. At Waitangi itself local tribal spokesmen often make speeches dealing with current issues, but in the rest of the country celebration revolves around festivals and concerts, with some *marae* (Maori meeting places) having an open day to explain Maori culture and the way forward for Maori.

BRITISH LEGACY

While both New Zealand and Australia were settled by Britain, it is New Zealand that more readily acknowledges, and is proud of, its British ancestry. At the turn of the twentieth century it was still very

British, with 20 percent of its population born in the UK; now the figure is closer to 6 percent. The people were considered "more English than the English," or, as the writer Anthony Trollope put it, "more John Bullish than John Bull." New Zealand, he said, considered herself the "cream" of the British Empire, although he had found this pretension in every colony he had visited. New Zealand still feels quite strongly about the Queen, still celebrates her official birthday, and has not taken any steps down the Republican route, as Australia has. It was the most dutiful of dominions. Some said that New Zealand liked to maintain its dependency on the old country because that way it could be part of a larger, more powerful commonwealth, but this situation has today greatly changed. Typically British, the first settlers in the islands thought that the blessings of their civilization should be imposed on those unlucky enough not to have been born into it. British immigrants came to New Zealand from varying backgrounds and at different times, bringing different values with them, along with the constants of fish and chips and democracy; tastes and values that have stuck!

BRITISH IMMIGRATION

In the early nineteenth century, people born in Britain were to be found in both the colony's elite and in the settler population. From 1854 to 1890, nearly half of the MPs holding office were British. The earliest settlers until the 1890s were from three main areas of southern England—London and Middlesex, the home counties of the southeast, and the southwest. Immigration from the London area usually followed slumps in various industries, particularly the construction industry, so laborers and skilled craftsmen, and also single women hoping for better marriage prospects in New Zealand's mostly male population, made up this segment. Immigration from England's

FIRST SCOTTISH
COLONY for
New Zealand

That Fine
Fast
SAILING

TEAK-BUILT

SHIP

BENGAL MERCHANT,
401 Tons Register—JOHN HEMERY, COMMANDER,
WILL POSITIVELY
SAIL FROM PORT-GLASGOW
For NEW ZEALAND,
With the first Body of Settlers
FROM SCOTLAND,
On FRIDAY, Oct. 25.

SINGLE WOMEN, going out as Servants to Cabin Passengers, or in charge of Married Emigrants, will receive a *Free Passage* on board of this Ship.
All Goods and Luggage must be forwarded by the 20th instant *at latest*, on which day the Ship will clear out.
For *Freight* (having room for dead Weight and Measurement Goods) and *Passage*, apply to
JOHN CRAWFORD,
22, QUEEN STREET.

NEW ZEALAND LAND Co's. OFFICE,
GLASGOW, 5th Oct. 1839.

southeastern rural counties followed a decline in wages and worsening conditions in the region. The failure in 1874 of the farm laborers' "revolt of the field"—protesting against the reduced wages and unemployment caused by the lower prices of foreign wheat, which signaled an end to the golden age of British agriculture—led to many leaving for colonial shores. These were not just farmworkers, but also craftsmen such as shoemakers and wheelwrights who could not compete with factory output. Similarly, the slump in copper and tin mining, worsened by imports from America, prompted those in the southwestern counties to leave.

At the end of the nineteenth and early twentieth centuries northern England become a source of new migrants. Again this resulted from unemployment, after 1920 in the shipbuilding, textile, and mining industries. In 1922 the British government subsidized family emigration and the New Zealand government permitted New Zealanders to nominate a person in England for assistance in migration. This scheme recruited industrial workers. Most of the last main wave of English, from the 1940s to 1975, came from the London area and northern England.

It was thus not difficult for English immigrants to become assimilated and, when many returned to England (it is thought that this was about one-third), those who remained became the target of some teasing from older settlers, who regarded the newer arrivals as "effete, new chums." This progressed to "moaning homies" in the 1920s, and "whingeing Poms" after the Second World War. Because of the varying backgrounds of the British settlers, they were regarded either as "a bit above themselves" or as union stirrers. Generally though, the British have adapted well to New Zealand, and have developed a great attachment to their new country. Of the many Europeans who arrive to settle every year, three-quarters are British.

British Culture and Traditions

The British brought with them traditions and customs, as well as associations and organizations such as fire brigades, local militia, building societies, brass bands, and the friendly societies, which helped the sick or bereaved before the Social Security Act of 1938. They played a prominent part in trade union activity, and contributed to the beginnings of the Labour Party.

British influence was also felt in the culinary area, with New Zealand's cooking based almost exclusively on Britain's. It is thanks to European immigrants arriving after the Second World War that fish and chips, "meat and two veg," cakes, puddings, sandwiches, and cups of tea have been augmented by greater variations in diet. The pie, though, is still popular fare, and a survey in 2001 found that fish and chips was the most popular fast food, despite the influence of the American chains, which found their way to New Zealand in the 1960s. Beer, which is still New Zealand's most popular alcoholic drink, was first brewed commercially in the country by a Londoner Joel Polack, who founded a brewery at Russell. Speights beer owes its origin to a Yorkshireman James Speight, who with partners from Devon and Scotland started a brewery in Dunedin. Today,

though, Kiwis usually ask for lagers served cold rather than the warm beer preferred by the early British settlers.

As far as TV and film are concerned, British programs such as "Top Gear," "Downton Abbey," and "Coronation Street" are favorites, but the trend, as it is worldwide, is to programs with a more American content. New Zealand has Britain to thank for its pantomimes, church music, including Christmas carols, and musical events such as the Proms music festival and concerts in the parks. The British tradition of country fairs and shows can be seen in what Kiwis call "A and P" (agricultural and pastoral) shows, which most rural towns put on annually. They have evolved, since first started in the 1840s, from being showcases for farmers to show their stock and produce and compete for prizes, to include more commercial entertainment. The shows usually last over a weekend or longer, and include equestrian events and activities such as woodcutting contests, in which Kiwis compete to see who can axe through a tree stump the fastest. Arts and crafts and entertainments for children, make it a good outing for the whole family.

There is no doubt that most of the sports played in New Zealand are of British origin (see Chapter 5). Organized sports with rules, governing bodies, and interclub competitions, have long been established

in the country. Soccer has gained in popularity, particularly since the Second World War, when more enthusiasts arrived from Britain. It had been slow to take off because few immigrants to the new country came from the Midlands area of England, where soccer originated. Horse racing has developed in the country, with the first formal meeting being held at the Bay of Islands in 1835. Today New Zealand thoroughbreds are valued worldwide for their superior bloodstock.

Early architecture also reflects British influence, and the 1850s saw buildings erected reminiscent of what had been left behind. Remnants of the Gothic revival style, as designed by English architects Benjamin Mountfort and Frederick Thatcher, can still be seen in a few older colonial homes, or "villas," as they are called in New Zealand.

However, while New Zealanders "must daily Americanize," as believed by Thomas

Cholmondeley, an Englishman who returned to England, his observation in 1854 that "the New Zealander will retain more of the Briton than any other colonist," appears to be still true today. The UK, especially London, is still the first stop for most young Kiwis on their "OE" (overseas experience), but their feeling toward the "Mother Country" can be somewhat critical, considering the average "Pom" as either "snobbish" or "yobbish," depending on whom they meet. The erosion in the status by the UK government of its Commonwealth members has soured that "special" relationship felt by New Zealanders. The recent implementation of a health charge of £200 on New Zealanders visiting the UK while visitors from Britain to New Zealand are entitled to free healthcare is seen as, according the NZ Prime Minister, "a chipping away of New Zealanders' rights in the UK."

RIVALRY AND RELATIONS WITH AUSTRALIA

The ongoing rivalry with Australia can vary from good-natured banter to a little more hostility—the gist being that to the Australians Kiwis are "hicks," and not really in the world, while to the New Zealanders Aussies are of inferior stock, mainly because of their convict origins. Australians also call Kiwis "South Seas Poms," because of what is perceived as their closer relationship with Britain, while Kiwis consider Aussies loud and opinionated. An Australian columnist's summing-up was that, "While we don't exactly hate New Zealanders we're not exactly fond of each other.

While they regard us as vulgar yobbos, almost Yank-like, we think of them as second-hand, recycled Poms." The patriotic theme is epitomized by the Kiwi in Australia who says, "I did not come to Oz, I just left New Zealand," while the Aussie counterpart said that he was going back to Oz because it rained so much in New Zealand and the place "badly needs roofing in." It is usually the Kiwis who make the more nationalistic comments, and this probably stems from the fact that New Zealand was once an Australian colony and ruled from Sydney by British governors.

Be that as it may, it is recognized that they are relatives, "cousins" or "brothers" being the popular portrayal, and carry on much as families do, with affection and quarrelsomeness being integral to the relationship. New Zealand's relationship with Australia—from an economic, social, and security viewpoint—is its most important. Australia until very recently was New Zealand's largest market and strongest trading partner, and the two countries have similar foreign and trading policies. They join together in times of trouble. Aussies contributed significantly to the New Zealand Labour cabinet in the 1930s, which comprised six Aussies, five Kiwis, an Englishman, and a Scot. One of New Zealand's most beloved Prime Ministers was Micky Savage, who was born an Australian.

Indeed, the number of New Zealanders living in Australia is so great (estimated at over 550,000, while only 63,000 Australians live in New Zealand) that New Zealand politicians canvass in Australia for votes. The Trans-Tasman arrangement of

1973 between the two countries allowed for free movement across the Tasman Sea, with each nationality being allowed to live and work in the other country without restrictions, although, in reality, fewer Australians took advantage of this. Consequently those Kiwis choosing to live in Australia were often accused of taking Aussie jobs or living off welfare benefits, although, since 2001, New Zealanders are barred from applying for citizenship and denied access to an ever-increasing number of government services. New Zealanders often complain that the Aussies poach New Zealand's best brains, and many Oz headhunting agencies recruit Kiwi medical and educational professionals, and also members of the New Zealand police force.

A joining of the two countries has often been mooted, but, ever since New Zealand declined to become Australia's seventh state in 1901, opinion polls have shown that New Zealanders are still totally against the idea, while the Australian government has expressed little interest.

Nevertheless, he two nations have much in common, including their former colonial ties with England and their inheritance of the British system of government, their support of Britain during two world wars, their alignment with the USA during the Cold War, participation in both the Korean and Vietnam Wars, and their relative isolation from the rest of the world. While their relationships with Britain have declined into more of a love–hate affair, Australia is far more republican than New Zealand, which continues to support the monarchy. More recently, in 1999, both countries were involved with the UN in the peacekeeping force for East Timor. But it was only Australia that went to war in the 2003 invasion of Iraq.

It is in sports where their rivalry surfaces, particularly in cricket and rugby, the two games that have become part of each nation's identity. Australian Trevor Chappell's "unsportsmanlike" underarm delivery, for instance, has never been forgiven by New Zealand's cricketing enthusiasts.

However, underneath all the differences of opinion and ongoing grievances, they defend one another—the Anzac tradition being the most significant example—and, when abroad, ally as Antipodeans against the rest. But get them on the rugby field, and it's war!

MAORI CULTURE

Maori culture is an inextricable part of New Zealand's identity. As original inhabitants they are known as *tangata whenua*, "people of the land," although their name is derived from *Ma-Uri*, which means "children of Heaven." Maori comprise many *iwi* (tribes), *hapu* (subtribes), and *whanau* (extended family units). Having originated in Polynesia, they brought with them the rich culture of the region, where song, dance, art, and oratorical skills are significant, especially as there was no written language at the time. Much of Maori history and myth has been passed on in this way. This sometimes gave rise to a blurring of fact and fiction, especially when some license was taken in adapting Polynesian folklore in order to make circumstances in the new country more comprehensible and relevant. Knowledge was often conveyed, too, by reciting *whakapapa,* or "genealogies."

The concepts of *mana* (status) and *utu* (reciprocity, payment, or revenge) are central to Maori culture. Status came from one's ancestors, who provided guidance and spiritual strength when called upon. In the past, warfare and violence often resulted, although this was, largely, episodic as most of the time Maori lived in unprotected *pa,* or "settlements," and seasonal camps. The *pa* originally resembled British Iron Age forts, and developed into more effective defenses with trenches and pits when Maori encountered the British. Today there are mostly only traces of these *pa* to be seen—in Auckland at the best lookout areas, such as Mount Eden and One Tree Hill, where the city's numerous volcanic cones made ideal sites; the Bay of Islands, in the Maritime and Historic Park; and in the Hawke's Bay at Otatara Pa Historic Reserve.

Maori Beliefs

Their relationship with the environment and their belief in deities and *atua* (spirits) have given rise to a set of belief systems that are inherent in the Maori social structuring of *tapu,* meaning "sacred" or "holy" (from which "taboo" originated and introduced to the British people by Captain Cook). There was a very strict division between certain things that were *tapu* and others that were *naa* (without sacred or holy power). For instance, cooked food was not permitted in the sacred *marae* area because it was *naa*.

Maori believe in divine direction in all matters, a legacy from their Polynesian past, where religion is closely related to nature. Their store of myth and legend is rich and explains the creation of the universe, its gods, people, and animals that inhabit it. Hence, in the beginning, it was Rangi (sky) and Papa (earth), the father and mother of all gods, who were parents to a host of other gods such as Tane, the god of trees and birds, Tawhiri, the god of winds, and Tangaroa, the god of the sea. All these gods are remembered through song and dance, and the rules they laid down by

which Maori would live were passed on through *tohunga ahurewa*, or earthly priests, who were very influential in the community. They tell the story of how the trickster Maui fished up New Zealand and how he found fire (from the underworld!); how the stars came into being from the tears of Uru, the forgotten child of Rangi and Papa. In his sadness, Uru would weep, filling baskets with his tears, and when the baskets were opened by his brother, Tane

HOW THE KIWI LOST HIS WINGS

One day, so the story goes, Tane Mahuta, the lord of the forest, was surveying his ferny domain and became concerned that his children, the trees, were ill from being eaten by bugs. He called the birds together to ask if any might be prepared to eat the bugs, which would entail living on the dark, damp forest floor.

Not surprisingly, he was met with reluctance. Most preferred flying around in the sunny sky above. The *tui*'s excuse was that he was afraid of the dark, the *pukeko* didn't want to get his feet wet, and the *pipiwharauroa* was preoccupied with building a nest. But the Kiwi put himself forward.

Tane Mahuta reminded him that he would never see daylight again, he would lose all his beautiful feathers, and he would grow thick, strong legs, which he would need for ripping open the fallen trees. The Kiwi agreed to do the job, and as a reward for his sacrifice became the best-known and most-loved bird of all.

The other birds did not fare so well. The *tui* was forced to wear two white feathers on his throat as the mark of a coward, the *pukeko* would live forever in a swamp, and the *pipiwharauroa* would never have another nest of her own, but would have to lay her eggs in those of other birds.

Mahuta, they had become dancing, bright lights,
or *purapurawhetu*, which Tane Mahuta scattered
all over the sky so that he would not be lonely in
the dark.

Rituals and Protocol

As Maori have a close relationship with their ancestors,
it is not surprising that *tangihanga*, or funerals, are
significant in the Maori tradition. Wakes continue for
several days, with relatives and acquaintances expected
to attend from all over the country. The farewell to
the dead includes not only ritual and songs, but also
myths and legends, which are passed on to the younger
generation and so perpetuated, and possibly slightly
changed, with each telling.

There is a strict, formal protocol whereby visitors
are welcomed into the *marae*, the sacred meeting
area, with its *whare runanga*, or meeting house,
which is the focus for community identity and
where all ceremonies are held. It traditionally faces
east to catch the sun's first rays. Each *marae* has its
own *tapu*, and strangers must wait to be invited
in. The signal for entry is a woman's high-pitched
call to the ancestors, a traditional recognition of
the spirits that takes place before any meeting, and
visitors should bow their heads as a mark of respect
for the dead. There are speeches of welcome and
ceremonial chants and then the greeting of the *hongi*,
the gentle pressing (note, not rubbing!) of noses and
forehead, and the *haka*, the challenging war dance
and chant. In former times, this was used to test
visitors' intentions—rivals would be frightened by

the warriors' might, while others were called upon to prove they were coming in peace.

Permission must always be asked before entering a *marae*. An organized visit is usually available for tourists, and this provides an ideal opportunity to learn something about Maori history, culture, and mythology. Visitors are received with a *powhiri*, or formal welcome, which begins with the *wero*, or challenge, when a traditionally dressed warrior, complete with *taiaha* (spear), will lay down a token for the guests to pick up, to indicate their peaceful intentions. Women will then perform the *kauranga*, or song of welcome. Inside, there will be greetings, speeches, and possibly more chanting and singing before the *hongi*.

It is important to be aware that some Maori sites are *tapu*, particularly the burial grounds, and should not be touched. Before entering the *marae*, all footwear must be removed. Don't smoke, eat, drink, or chew gum, and don't sit on any surfaces such as tables, where food may be prepared or eaten. Don't take photographs of Maori buildings unless you have ensured that you are permitted to do so, as the *marae* is an important and sacred part of Maori life, and should be accorded appropriate respect.

Art Forms

The Maori tradition of carving, used for adorning important wooden buildings and canoes, is significant, as is the fashioning of stone into tools and ornaments. The purpose of the carvings is not only decorative, but also to reflect the deep respect in which ancestors are held. Such art forms extend to carved walking sticks, engravings on bone, and greenstone necklaces, which are of great importance to Maori because they carry the spirit of the original owners. Throughout every *marae* the wooden *whakapapa* is carefully carved, with the dominant figure a human with a protruding tongue. If you have seen the All Blacks perform the *haka* before any match you will recognize the stance.

Despite Western influence and the fact that nearly 500,000 Maori now live in cities, the tribal connection is maintained, especially with the recent resurgence of Maori culture. Rituals and ceremonies are still carried out using the traditional music and dance, and Maori traditions and art forms have become *taonga*, or national treasures.

Tattoos

Since 1500 BCE the practice of tattooing has been an integral part of the Tahitian culture from which Maori originated; it is also significant in Maori culture. The word "tattoo" derives from the Tahitian *tatau*, meaning "open wound." While today it is a popular form of adornment worldwide, tattooing is treated by Maori with reverence, as it perpetuates history, conveys identity, and preserves culture. Not

surprisingly, Maoris have a story about how tattooing was brought from the underworld by Mataora, a handsome young chief. It seems that he had been there to look for a wife, but came back with a tattoo instead.

Originally it was usually only the face that was adorned with a tattoo, or *moko,* as it is called by the Maori. It was applied with a wood carving technique. A chisel-like bone was dipped in a pigment made from the soot of burnt candlenut mixed with water and oil. A wooden stick was then used to tap the bone against the skin, so puncturing it. This practice was banned twenty years ago, and today artists use a machine, developed from an electric shaver, to eliminate the risk of disease. Tattoo designs were similar to those used in other art forms, such as wood carving, with many designs taken from nature. Only men could have a full-face *moko,* while females were permitted to decorate only the chin, upper lip, and nostrils.

In Maori culture, the design of a traditional tattoo will impart details about the bearer such as tribal affiliations and origins, family, and social status; a person of higher rank would have more tattoos. Sometimes the right to bear a specific tattoo has to be earned. In older days it was said that a man without a *moko* was a *papatea,* or "plain face," meaning a "nobody." *Moko* originated when Maori warriors, who painted their faces with charcoal before battles to frighten the enemy, decided to make the lines more permanent. Although full-face *moko* died out at the end of the 1800s, tattooing has reemerged in New Zealand and also in the rest of the world. Maori-inspired patterns and designs have become immensely popular fashion statements for men and women, with celebrities such as Rihanna, Mike Tyson, and Robbie Williams prominently displaying their decorations.

chapter four

DAILY LIFE

HOME IS NOT ALWAYS WHERE THE HEART IS
Although New Zealand has slowly become more
prosperous, owning one's home is not the dream of
every Kiwi. The number of homeowners has fallen since
the 1980s, when 74 percent of the population owned
their homes. Today only 50 percent are homeowners.
This is probably attributable to income tax changes at
that time, as well as cuts in social security benefits in the
1990s, which also saw higher unemployment. The gap

between rich and poor widened, and 80 percent of people suffered declines in income, largely because of the slump in the economy. Today approximately one-third of New Zealanders rent rather than own their homes.

Maori and Pacific Islanders are more likely to live in rented accommodation, while Europeans usually own their own homes, often without a mortgage, although this is largely due to this population having had more time to pay it off. Property prices have soared over the last few years, with a nationwide average house price for the month of July 2015 of NZ $527,760. Property values are up 10 percent over the past year and are now over 25 percent above the previous market peak of late 2007, putting home ownership out of reach for many. Mortgage rates in 2015 averaged around 6 percent per annum, with more than 65 percent of households electing for fixed-rate rather than floating loans since the former became widely offered in 1994. More than half of the approximately 1,780,000 privately owned dwellings are mortgaged.

Three-quarters of New Zealanders live in urban areas with populations of at least 10,000. The rural population consists mainly of Europeans and Maori, rather than Asians or Pacific Islanders, who prefer large cities where the work is, particularly Auckland, where one-third of the population was born overseas. In contrast, in the South Island only one in fifteen people was born out of the country. Half the country's population is concentrated in the cities of Auckland, Hamilton, and Wellington in the North Island, and

Christchurch in the South Island. The population of the northern area of the North Island has grown faster than that of the South Island, probably as a result of immigration and the higher birthrates among the Maori and Pacific Islanders rather than internal migration.

The government has initiated a number of projects to provide affordable housing to New Zealanders. The Housing New Zealand Corporation, which was established under a government Act of 1974, provides housing and related services. Programs include Community Group Housing, which supplies accommodation for those with special needs; Healthy Housing, whose objective is to reduce overcrowding and health risks; Low Deposit Rural Lending, whereby families with low incomes, particularly Maori, are assisted with loans for home ownership; Rural Housing, which helps those in substandard homes to effect repairs, and to ensure proper sanitation, electricity, and other basic requirements; Maintenance of the State Housing Portfolio, whereby state assets are maintained and modernized; and Home Ownership, which is a mortgage insurance scheme to help those on low incomes.

Eighty percent of all private dwellings across both islands are detached homes housing single families, but multiunit homes are increasing, mainly due to lack of space, particularly in Auckland. There has been a gradual increase in the number of larger homes with four or more bedrooms, indicative of increased wealth and income inequalities. Houses are usually single-story, wooden, often on stilts in hilly areas and, in the Kiwi manner, practical, although recent years have seen greater emphasis on design.

Much of New Zealand's architecture has been influenced by overseas trends, evolving from styles reminiscent of what the immigrants had left behind to those with a more European or American look. These were adapted to suit the environment, hence the accent on timber because of its ready availability and adaptability to the climate and informal Kiwi lifestyle. These wooden houses also have the

advantage of being movable, and it is not unusual to see houses being transported on special carriers to their owners' new site, or block, as it is called. Colonial-style houses with a lot of old-world charm, called villas, are scattered around. Some impressive nineteenth-century houses may be visited—a list of historic homes can be obtained from the local i-SITE Visitor Information Centre, easily found in most cities and towns.

The "Bach"

Many New Zealanders have a vacation home, commonly called a "bach" in most of the country and a "crib" in Otago and Southland. Its character has changed from a basic shelter to a home on an altogether grander scale. It was usually made of cheap materials, such as recycled timber, or corrugated iron, and the now-banned asbestos. The name derives from "bachelor," and probably dates from the early days of men-only fishing trips when only essentials were required and any furniture was practical rather than aesthetic. Many early baches were erected illegally on beach property, which is owned by the government, and while those built before a certain date have been permitted to remain, new buildings or modifications to existing ones have not been allowed. Baches mostly came on the scene after the Second World War, when Kiwis became more prosperous. The original ones had rainwater tanks and primitive lavatories known as "dunnies" or "long drops." Nowadays, however, Kiwi baches are architect-designed and have become much more sophisticated. Consequently, they have lost a lot of their original character and heritage to become just another vacation or second home.

The Shed

Two things make up the essence of being a "good Kiwi bloke," and these are playing rugby and having a shed. Kiwis are a practical nation and a bunch of "do-it-yourselfers," so usually they have a workshop of some kind—a "shed"—in which they will often mend anything from cars to washing machines and lawnmowers as a further source of income. So great is the tradition of the shed that there is even a society dedicated to them. MENZSHED New Zealand, set up in 2013, provides information to those interested and passionate about men's sheds in New Zealand.

Garage Sales

Related to the home environment is the garage sale, which is held when a Kiwi moves or simply wants to clear out some belongings, working on the premise that one person's junk is another's treasure. Some homeowners have them on a regular basis. They are usually held on a Saturday morning and advertised in the local newspaper and Internet, often listing the major items on offer. Practitioners in this art are careful to add the words "not before [a certain time]" in their advertisement, which may put off a few from arriving too early, but does not prevent many from lining up and then surging in when the garage door is opened at the appointed time. Many people go from one sale to another just looking to see what the neighbors are throwing out, but garage sales can be a useful source for those wanting secondhand goods for the minimum outlay.

"Shifting" and "Going Walkabout"

New Zealanders move or, as they term it, "shift" a lot. The average Kiwi moves every five years and it is not unusual to see several realtors in even a small town.

Kiwis also go "walkabout". Unlike the Australian meaning of going into the outback, in New Zealand, the word has developed to describe the Kiwi want or

need for a break or change in their lives. For this the mobile home has become what might be called their vehicle of opportunity.

So popular is this trend that New Zealanders convert buses into sophisticated homes on wheels complete with wood-burning fires, microwaves, and TV. A few months' break often lengthens into a few years, and such travelers have formed their own club with groups of "roadies," as they call themselves, meeting up regularly at favorite spots throughout the country.

Local rules on "Freedom Camping" —the parking of a camper by a lake or a river—vary in each area of New Zealand and should be checked at the i-SITE Visitors Center or consult the *Official Camping Map of New Zealand.* You can often find that the beauty of a particular lake or mountain is yours alone to appreciate and savor. However, if you choose to camp in a non-designated camping area then leave no trace of your visit, Kiwis are fastidious about protecting their environment.

Boats and "Tinnies"

New Zealand being a nation of islanders, it is not surprising that boats and boating feature strongly in the Kiwi way of life, and boats of various shapes and sizes fill driveways, gardens, and garages. It is said that one in three New Zealanders owns a boat of some sort. These can range from yachts and "gin palaces" to the simple "tinny." The latter is an affectionate term reserved for a small rowing boat made of aluminium.

Fishing goes back over a thousand years in New Zealand, dating to when the Polynesians first came and fish was a vital source of food. *Kai mona*, "food from the sea," is still important to Maori, who use lines or nets and also collect mussels, *pipi*, and *paua*. This last is abalone, or perlemoen, which has the added attraction of its decorative inner shell of opalescent greens and blues, used in jewelry and souvenirs. The shell is also culturally significant to Maori.

Fishing is a very popular pastime, and fishermen can be seen wherever there may be fish—dangling a hand line off a bridge in a more populated area; trying

to catch salmon, perch, or trout in freshwater lakes and rivers (fly-fishing here is recognized as being among the world's best); surf casting off the shores and rocks of New Zealand's ample coastline for snapper, *terakihi*, or *kawhau*; or simply cruising the ocean where big game fishing for tuna and marlin is particularly good off the north coast in the Pacific.

The Bay of Islands was a favorite haunt of western writer Zane Gray, who has a café named after him on the island of Urupukapuka. Everyone has a rod of sorts, and children are encouraged to fish from an early age, with competitions frequently held to maintain their enthusiasm. This certainly has had its effect on the female population. New Zealand must be one of the few countries in the world where women go off on "girls only" fishing weekends.

Everyone who fishes recreationally in New Zealand has a legal requirement to follow the recreational fishing rules. New Zealand has seven fishing areas and you need to follow the specific rules for the area where you're fishing. As the rules change regularly you will need to check every time you embark on a trip.

EDUCATION

Numeracy and literacy have recently become major political issues, particularly as international statistics have revealed that the gap between New Zealand's best and worst achievers is greater than anywhere else in the developed world. It is estimated that 25 percent of New Zealand students (around 12,000

SOME KIWIANA

These are the things that contribute to being a Kiwi. Some of them are also Australian, and evoke nostalgia in those from both countries when away from home!

- Buzzy Bee—a child's toy in colors of red and yellow
- No. 8 wire—an all-purpose wire, symbol of Kiwi ingenuity and adaptability
- Pavlova—a dessert of fruit and cream on a generous meringue base
- Vogel's bread—a full grain bread
- Jandals—thonged sandals, or flip-flops
- Paua shell ashtrays
- L & P—a lemonade type drink that has become the national soft drink
- Anzac Biscuits— rolled oats and golden syrup cookies
- Vegemite—a yeast spread, based on the UK's Marmite
- A and P (agricultural and pastoral) shows
- Bluff Oysters—the best oysters in the country, caught off the coast around Bluff, in the South Island
- Lamingtons—sponge cakes with chocolate icing and rolledin dessicated coconut
- Black gum boots— rubber boots

per annum) leave school without adequate skills to become competent citizens. New Zealand's educational structure has been decentralized, with schools and tertiary establishments becoming autonomous within guidelines set by government. Education is free for pupils from five to nineteen years of age, and compulsory between the ages of six and sixteen. Many state schools do, however, ask parents to contribute to school expenses that the state does not fund. Children usually start school at the age of five, although many attend kindergartens, or play or childcare centers before this age. Sixty percent of children under age five participate in early education, and this includes 90 percent of three-year-olds and 98 percent of four-year-olds.

The school day for primary students usually starts at 9:00 a.m. and finishes at 3:00 p.m.; secondary schools start earlier and finish later. The school year runs from February to December and has four terms. Each term is roughly ten weeks long. Summer holidays last about five and a half weeks at primary schools and about a week longer at secondary schools. The fall, winter and spring holidays each last two weeks.

State schools at primary and intermediate level are coeducational, as are most secondary schools. They are governed by boards of trustees elected by the parents. Primary schooling is from years one to six, intermediate covers years seven and eight, and secondary years nine to thirteen. In some schools intermediate level is combined with either primary or secondary. Although today pupils are staying on longer at school, fewer Maori stay until age eighteen. Most Maori are educated within the state system, although they have their own free schools, where the Maori language is preserved and education is based on Maori culture and traditional values.

There are also integrated state schools and private schools. The former arose after the state established a secular system of education in 1877. The Roman Catholic Church, for instance, instituted its own separate system of schools, which has now been integrated into the state system but are still permitted to retain their own character as long as entrance to the school is open. Private schools, usually church established, do not integrate with the state and have elected to maintain their independence, being governed by their own boards. As fee-paying institutions (although there is some state funding), many have become socially elite.

There are thirty-six higher education establishments throughout the country. These include eight universities, twenty-three institutes of technology and polytechnics, four colleges of education, and three Maori institutions, called *wananga,* which offer a wide spectrum of higher studies to master's level but with a Maori influence, some having a more trade and technical orientation than purely academic. There are also forty-six organizations that provide education in specific sectors of industry, and approximately nine hundred private training establishments, which include English-language schools.

The tertiary academic year follows the state school calendar with four terms commencing in late January and finishing in mid-December. Teacher education is

offered at colleges of education as well as at some universities, institutes of technology, polytechnics, and private training institutions. Students pay a contribution toward fees for most courses, but a loan scheme makes higher education more easily accessible. The education of foreign students, particularly those from Southeast Asia, has become a major source of export earnings.

The National Certificate of Educational Achievement is the graduation qualification at secondary level. NCEA can be gained at three levels, which correspond to the last three years of secondary schooling. It is awarded when a number of credits have been achieved; university qualification requires forty-two credits, for example. Its introduction has been controversial as the two types of national standards—unit and achievement—have caused some confusion and the grade levels of "pass," "merit," and "excellence" have been considered too general to be meaningful, the concern being that it permits many who would not normally have qualified to do so. Hence many private schools take the English "A" levels or International Baccalaureate as well as the NCEA. A quarter of New Zealanders over the age of fifteen have no educational qualification, while one in eight has a university degree.

SHOPS AND BANKS

Shopping hours in New Zealand vary, but generally speaking stores open at 9:00 a.m. and close between 5.00 and 5:30 p.m., Monday to Saturday. In the larger towns and cities there are later opening hours, and on Sundays for limited hours. Some supermarkets stay open until 8:00 p.m., and some are open all night. Many shops, which cater to tourists, are open every day, often with extended hours. Although there is a move to supermarkets, the "dairy," or convenience

store, is still very much a presence, often remaining open on weekends and evenings for workers.

Banks are usually open from 9:30 a.m. to 4:30p.m., Monday to Friday, and are closed over the weekend. The banking system is advanced, and there is a large network of ATMs and EFTPOS (Electronic Funds Transfer at Point of Sale) facilities in most shops. Additionally, most overseas credit cards can be used at ATMs providing you have a four-digit pin number. Although credit cards are usually acceptable throughout the country, smaller retailers may not carry facilities and some may have a minimum purchase amount.

New Zealand is known as a country of "specials," and this is particularly noticeable in supermarkets. Many items, and often meat, are sold more cheaply if the sell-by date is imminent (and it is a good idea to check the date even on other, non-bargain items). "Specials" on beer and wine occur from time to time, and also on perishables. Outlets such as sushi bars, where freshness is essential, often sell at half-price at the end of the day. Strict advertising laws ensure that the price displayed is the price paid. Prices are not normally negotiable, though some retailers do have a policy of matching or beating competitive products, and some will give discounts on items such as electronics and appliances, particularly to those buying several products. You have nothing to lose by asking!

All goods and services are subject to a 15 percent Goods and Services Tax (GST). This is included in the displayed price of an item. Visitors cannot claim this tax back when a supplier ships a major purchase to a visitor's home address as the GST will not be charged.

TELEVISION AND OTHER MEDIA

Radio broadcasting commenced in New Zealand in 1922. Television was introduced only in 1960, with color TV not arriving until the 1970s, which also saw the arrival of more local content, particularly drama series and the ever-popular soap operas. Deregulation in the 1980s saw an increase in both radio and TV stations. There are three major free-to-air TV channels and over two hundred radio stations, including two national noncommercial stations. Most hotels and motels have TV with the three national channels and local TV, and some also provide Sky. Sky Network's digital transmission is also available to subscribers, with a number of packages on offer. Maori TV, funded by the government, started broadcasting in 2004, and there are many local TV stations covering regional news dotted throughout the country.

Free-to-air digital television and digital radio is available throughout New Zealand via satellite. Freeview's terrestrial service Freeview UHF aerial is a high definition digital terrestrial television service available to 75 percent of the country's population, using DVB-S and DVB-T standards on government provided spectrum. New Zealanders have benefited immensely from the arrival of digital television. Reception in the past was notoriously poor due to the country's challenging topography. The old analogue system was switched off in 2013.

There are very many private radio stations, including twenty-one Maori stations and a national Maori-language news service, while Pacific Island and other immigrant and community groups have started their own services. The government retains National Radio, Concert FM, Radio New Zealand external services, and a parliamentary broadcasting service.

TV and radio programs are listed daily in the newspapers and on the Internet. The trend today is toward talk shows, and several broadcasters have made a name for themselves in this area by airing controversial topics for discussion by telephone call-ins. These "talk-back" radio programs often include interviews with politicians and experts in different fields, who all clearly recognize the influence that these shows have. Tuning in to such programs gives visitors an idea of issues of concern to the average Kiwi and where his priorities lie. Similarly there are daily current affairs shows on TV. Be warned, however, that news items can sometimes be dragged out over days, and a common fault is that everyone connected with a particular story, however remotely, is interviewed.

While children still spend a lot of time watching TV, the computer has become more pervasive, and computers and play stations can be found in most households. Kiwis have become very Internet-conscious, and bookings and purchases are frequently transacted in this way. E-mail, too, has taken off, although the postal service is very efficient. Cell phones, or mobiles, as they are called here, are prolific—in fact there are more per capita than in most other countries in the world.

Kiwis also read a lot. Despite the global downturn in the retail book industry, New Zealand had the lowest drop in book sales in comparison to all other English-speaking countries. In 2012 sales dropped by just 2.7 percent, while sales in its neighbor Australia dropped by 10.4 percent.

BECOMING A KIWI

The laws governing naturalization have changed considerably over the years. Up to 1986, immigration policy focused on nationality and ethnic origin for acceptance, but since then the emphasis has been on specific educational, professional, business, age, and skills requirements, regardless of nationality or race.

Immigrants are selected according to the three main categories of skills and business, family ties, and humanitarian reasons.

The system is designed to attract those immigrants most needed in the country, and this also serves to control numbers. Minimum standards of English are now required and, for the skilled migrant category and certain business categories, the level is the equivalent of university admittance. The process today is centered on a selection pool for which one qualifies by having a certain number of points, awarded according to age, qualifications, work experience, employment status, skills shortage in the country, and specific job offer. Applicants also have to be of good health and character, and all medical and X-ray certificates must be less than three months old at the time an application is filed.

The New Zealand Immigration Service now also applies much stricter rules, making it harder to get into the country if there is a troublesome medical history, including HIV/AIDS, TB, mental impairment where hospitalization is required, physical incapacity where full-time care is needed, or cases needing dialysis treatment. Current policy requires that an applicant not be a potential burden on the health service or present a threat to others, thus giving the Immigration Service considerable leeway in what constitutes the description of "healthy."

There is still encouragement of people in the skilled/business stream category—particularly of investors prepared to contribute a minimum of NZ

$1 million or Investor Plus applicants with at least
NZ $10 million to invest; entrepreneurs, who have
to prove establishment of a successful business in
New Zealand; employees of relocating businesses;
and those given the opportunity of establishing
a business as a basis for future residence. This
category usually provides up to 60 percent of new
immigrants.

The family-sponsored stream comprises
approximately 30 percent of total immigration
numbers, usually partners and dependent children,
while the international/humanitarian stream
makes up the remaining amount of 10 percent.
This latter category includes refugees and Pacific
Islanders given special access. In 2015 the top five
source countries for migrants was India, China, the
Philippines, UK, and Germany.

To qualify for citizenship, general rules involve
being a permanent resident with the intention
of continued residence (which often means
owning a house or business), being of good
character, speaking English, and understanding
the responsibilities and privileges of New Zealand
citizenship. Special ceremonies have to be attended
for one to obtain citizenship, which then entitles the
holder to a New Zealand passport.

chapter five

TIME OUT

By and large, New Zealanders do not have a great deal of leisure time. Many people hold down more than one job to make ends meet, sometimes carrying out small repair and servicing jobs in their sheds to add to their income. However, when they can grab some leisure time they usually prefer to be out and about—they are a great sporting nation. Fishing is a popular recreation even for those who do not have a boat or are unable to get to the sea—a river, even in the middle of town, will do. As Kiwis have become wealthier, so their pursuits have become more expensive, hence the growth of restaurants and wineries. Home entertaining is largely the preserve of the better-heeled Kiwi, and "barbies" are a favorite.

FOOD AND DRINK

New Zealand's cuisine has developed considerably from its early British roots. Food and cooking styles have been influenced and enriched by immigrants from all over the world and traditional Maori ingredients have become a regular feature in restaurants and home kitchens. The New Zealand climate means that vegetables such as aubergines (eggplant), zucchini, and *kumara* (the Maori word for sweet potato) are available, as well as the more traditional British repertoire of carrots, peas, and cauliflower. A visit to any of the major multicultural markets will reveal the extent

of the country's culinary diversity, where exotic, fresh, and inexpensive produce can be bought and even tasted beforehand. Otara Market in South Auckland and the Sunday market at Avondale to the west of the city are worth a visit. Here a range of Maori and other ethnic vegetables can be found.

With a 9320 mile (15,000 km) coastline and 1.7 square mile (4.4 sq. km) area of territorial waters, New Zealand has a thriving fishing industry. The main fish market, Auckland Fish Market, at Viaduct Harbor, sells seafood from all over New Zealand—large tanks sport live crayfish and mussels, while

masses of snapper, trevally, *tarakihi*, and tuna are also on offer. As New Zealand is apparently one of only three places in the world for a particular species of whitebait *īnanga* (the others

being Patagonia in South America and the southern
Australian coastline), it is worth trying these tiny
seasonal fish that are commonly found around both
islands, but spawn in a small number of bays off the
South Island. They are caught from early September
to mid November. Freshwater crayfish, also called
koura, are found in small numbers throughout the
country and are farmed in central Otago. Oysters,
too, are good, particularly Bluff oysters, which are
considered a great delicacy and are harvested from
March until June or July, depending on when the
yearly quota is reached. They live wild in the cold
waters of Foveaux Strait that separates the South
Island from Stewart Island. Their exquisite flavor is
celebrated at the Bluff Festival in May. Supermarkets
sell fresh shellfish, and their staff will always advise
on what is fresh and what has been frozen.

The merits of New Zealand lamb are
internationally recognized. The beef is also
outstanding, and the Wairarapa area on the North
Island is particularly well-known for its quality meat.
Farmed venison, or *cervena*, is becoming a popular
alternative for those looking for something different.

In larger towns there are weekend farmers markets
that sell seasonal produce. Typical of these are Napier
and Hastings in Hawke's Bay where, in spring, there
are strawberries and asparagus; in summer, berries
and stone fruit; and in fall, avocados and olive oil;
with citrus fruit in winter. Interesting and different
fruit includes the *feijoa*, which is mostly grown in
the Bay of Plenty, and has a distinctive aroma. It can
be eaten raw, on its own or added to fruit salad, or

peeled and baked with native Manuka honey, and it also makes delicious jam and chutney. Tamarillos, or tree tomatoes, originally from South America have become popular on restaurant menus.

Herbs are plentiful, with a big move to organic planting. Maori herbs include *pikopiko,* a fern frond similar to the European and American fiddlehead fern. *Horopito* is another herb, with peppery leaves, which is tasty on grilled fish and is also an ingredient in salad dressings.

New Zealand's cheese industry has boomed, and consumers are spoiled for choice. Kapiti cheese is renowned for its different varieties, and continues to be one of New Zealand's foremost specialty cheese makers, scooping many food awards. Try the creamy Kikorangi, soft white Kotuku and Camembert, Kapiti aged (and smoked) cheddar, and Kapiti Brick, a washed-rind variety. Many boutique cheese makers have concocted new products using goats' and ewes' milk.

Not to be forgotten is New Zealand's ever-popular dessert, Pavlova, whose variations are many. (There is some conjecture as to whether it was created in Australia or New Zealand.) The basic recipe is that of a meringue, crisp on the outside, with a softer, more marshmallow center, topped with whipped cream and fruit such as kiwi fruit, strawberries or passionfruit.

Mention should be made of Anzac biscuits (cookies), which are in every Kiwi larder. These are made from oatmeal bound with golden syrup, and are plain and hard to the bite. They were, of course, originally made for the Anzac troops in the First World War.

Along with natural produce, the variety of foodstuffs has increased greatly with over 2,000 specialty food manufacturers producing everyday and gourmet products for the local and international markets. Also significant and in keeping with the clean, green image of New Zealand is that many food producers are certified organic growers.

EDMONDS COOKERY— THE KIWI CULINARY BIBLE

In 1908, Thomas Edmonds, producer of Edmonds "Sure to Rise" Baking Powder published, as a give-away, a fifty-page booklet  of economical, everyday recipes and cooking hints using his product. Couples who announced their engagement in the paper received a free copy. Housewives who applied in writing would also receive a complimentary copy. With sales of well over 3.3 million copies, few New Zealanders are without one, and it has become a Kiwi tradition to be given a copy on first leaving home.

Wine

In matters of imbibing, New Zealanders have become much more sophisticated. Until the last century beer was very much the national drink with the annual consumption of wine per capita at just under one bottle, as against three liters (over six pints) of spirits and thirty-four liters (nearly seventy-two pints) of beer! Drinking habits changed in the nineties, and today the annual wine consumption per Kiwi is approximately twenty-one liters (forty pints).

The first vines were planted as early as 1819; since then number of wineries has increased considerably, and in 2013 there were 698. Even though vineyards are small by international standards, wine production is now an important export.

Because of the country's varying climate and soil, New Zealand produces a number of varietals from Sauvignon Blanc, Riesling, and Chardonnay, to Merlot and Cabernet, although it was Sauvignon Blanc that established New Zealand's reputation, particularly the wines from the Marlborough region in the South Island. In the last few years New Zealand's Pinot Noir has emerged as a best-seller on the international scene. The cooler nights and special sunlight in central Otago where it is produced.

It makes sense to try the wine of the region; even

smaller restaurants offer an adequate choice, and wine by the glass if the price of a bottle is discouraging.

Other varietals that compete internationally are Chenin Blanc, Gewurztraminer, Pinot Gris, Cabernet Franc, Malbec, and Syrah. A number of boutique wineries have also sprung up—Waiheke Island, east of Auckland, is such an area, as is the region around Warkworth on the way to the Bay of Islands. Martinborough in the Wairarapa near Wellington has its own wine festival each year. Buses tour around the town, ferrying people to the various wineries. This has now become so popular, and a bit of a social occasion, that tickets are sold out long before the event.

Although there are often "specials" on offer at supermarkets, a medium-range wine will set you back NZ $15 per bottle. It is perfectly acceptable to take wine under $15 if you are visiting friends—the Kiwis will not judge you on that—but it is not a good idea to take them Aussie wine! They don't mind trying Chilean, Hungarian, or French, but their Tasman neighbor is just too close a rival. Wine is only an everyday drink for the better off, the average Kiwi bloke still preferring a beer.

Be aware that there are liquor ban areas, in which alcoholic drinks cannot be consumed or even carried, in certain places such as city centers and beachfronts at certain times of day, particularly in resort areas over the summer vacation season. The police may ask you to empty bottles and arrest you if you do not comply.

It is perfectly safe to drink water from the tap
although some town supplies are drawn from river
water and chlorinated. Or as an alternative you could
try New Zealand's national soft drink L & P (Lemon
and Paeroa), a lemonade-type drink that was
originally made with the spring waters of Paeroa.

EATING OUT

New Zealand offers a wide variety of ethnic
restaurants, from Japanese, Vietnamese, and Korean
to the more customary French and Italian. New
flavors and products, particularly Asian ones,
compete with fusion and Pacific Rim cooking.

Savoury pies are probably still the nation's
favorite dish, but fish and chips come a close second.
New Zealand's restaurants compare favorably
with those of the rest of the world, but décor and
ambience are often lacking. Even upscale restaurants
can lack atmosphere, having more of a casual, café-
like feel. Sushi bars are very popular and you will
find one in most towns.

Despite a growing awareness of healthy eating,
there is no shortage of fast-food outlets. Offering
cheaper fare they are popular with the less well-off,
and Thursdays, when welfare payments are made.
sees a sharp rise in receipts.

Fish is good in New Zealand, although not
as cheap as one might expect. Snapper, the most
prolific fish, is possibly one of the more expensive
and one wonders why! Green-lipped mussels are
fleshy, succulent, and much more substantial than

the European equivalents, and abalone (*paua*) is also popular, particularly as fritters or even fresh as *sashimi*. Auckland boasts some of the country's best seafood restaurants, particularly in the Viaduct Harbor, but it is probably Wellington that has the more cosmopolitan establishments.

Dress for dining out is very informal. Most restaurants expect a tidy appearance, but few require suits and ties. There have been restrictions on smoking in public places since 1990. This was extended to a ban in bars and restaurants in 2004. Some bars now provide a covered outdoor area for the use of smokers.

"Bring Your Own"

As in Australia, many restaurants are BYO, or "bring your own bottle," and display this in their window and in their advertisements. Restaurants that have liquor licenses will usually let you bring your own bottle, although corkage is charged, and as this varies considerably it is a good idea to ascertain this in advance. Some more expensive restaurants will not permit BYO at all.

Trying Maori Fare

For more adventurous eaters, traditional Maori food can be experienced at Maori concert evenings, especially in the Rotorua area. Most visitors enjoy a *hangi,* originally a Polynesian practice, where food is cooked in an earth oven. This is really just a hole in the ground, which has been lined with hot rocks, whose steam cooks the wrapped food.

Layers of meat, fish, vegetables, and finally shellfish are covered with cabbage leaves, and soil is put on top. Cooking lasts a few hours, and the food is usually quite succulent, but it is a delicate art to get the timing right. Maori in the Rotorua district also boil food in hot pools. Another delicacy is *puha,* which is akin to watercress. Maori boil this up with pork bones and potatoes, which makes for a hearty winter dish, especially when accompanied by *rewena* bread. Sauces and relishes are also typical, and one particularly favored in the past combines a mixture of tastes, sweet and sour. It consists of several wild edibles —*tawhara* or *kiekie, tutu* juice—mixed with fuchsia berries, peaches, onions, sweet and ordinary potatoes, pig brains, and lard.

Another traditional food source is the mutton bird, a member of the petrel family. It got its colloquial name from the early European settlers, who preserved it in salt; when eaten, its oily flesh tasted similar to preserved mutton. Mutton bird is available alongside fresh fish in the larger supermarkets.

Café Culture

New Zealand is a café society, and even the smallest town will have several coffee bars. It has more coffee roasters per capita than anywhere in the world. People meet each other for coffee at the drop of a hat, and at all levels, although town coffee bars differ from rural ones and offer more choice. A lot of socializing is done in the cafés, and one often hears a Kiwi saying that she and her spouse are "just going

down the road for a coffee," or that she's "meeting the girls for a coffee." One is spoiled for choice by the different types of coffee to be had, and the quality is very good; tea appears to have lost its monopoly.

FLAT WHITE
New Zealand has gained the distinction among the world's coffee aficionados as pioneering the "flat white," which, according to Kiwi baristas, is a less milky brew with textured rather than frothy milk.

Table Manners
The polite way of eating follows the European custom of using a knife in the right hand and a fork in the left, throughout the meal. Utensils are rested on the plate during a pause, and, on finishing, knife and fork are

placed, tines pointing up and the knife parallel, in the middle of the plate. Kiwis are quite adept at using chopsticks, as sushi bars have become very popular. In some upscale restaurants, when serving a couple a waiter will usually ask for the order from the man, who will have ascertained his partner's choice. In most other situations, such as with a larger party, the waiter will attend to each person in turn, asking the women first. There are not really any hard or fast rules, though, as New Zealand is quite an informal and relaxed society.

TIPPING

Service charges and tips are not included in receipts and tipping is not a traditional New Zealand practice. However, in the major cities such as Auckland, tipping is becoming more common, especially in higher-end establishments, and 10 percent of the check is acceptable. Also be expected to pay an additional service charge on statutory holidays to cover the increase in staffing costs.

INVITATIONS HOME

Generally, New Zealanders do not readily invite you to their homes, but if they do it will probably be for an informal "barbie." It is usual to ask if you can contribute some meat, but if the offer is declined a bottle of wine will always be welcome. Chocolates and flowers are usually reserved for more formal occasions, like dinner parties.

You may be invited to join a few people one evening, and to "bring a plate." This does not mean that your hosts are running short of crockery! It means that everyone is contributing something toward the meal, and that you are expected to bring a dish of food. It is a good idea to ask what sort of "plate" they would like, to avoid duplicating what others are bringing.

It is worth noting some of the terminology. "Afternoon tea" is between 3:00 and 4:00 p.m., and means a cup of tea with cakes and cookies. Be aware, however, if you are asked for "tea," that this will usually mean an evening meal, and Kiwis usually eat early—about 6:00 to 8:00 p.m. "Supper" will mean a later evening snack.

SHOPPING
New Zealand has a Goods and Services Tax (GST) of 15 percent, which is charged on most goods and services and is usually included in the price unless otherwise stated. Visitors should note that tax paid on purchases made cannot be claimed back, and shopping at duty-free outlets is only possible on production of a passport and airline ticket or boarding pass. Other larger and top end retailers, such as department stores or art dealers, will not charge GST on any "larger ticket" items mailed to a home address outside New Zealand. It pays to check whether a store operates this system before buying.

CULTURAL PURSUITS

Theater, opera, and music are alive and well in New
Zealand, although they are generally not found
outside the major cities, and are usually the preserve
of the better-educated and the moneyed. However,
the free "Opera in the Park" and "Symphony under
the Stars," held in Auckland's Domain in the summer,
and to which many people bring picnics, are attended
by a wide spectrum of the public. Similarly, "Carols
by Candlelight" is a popular family outing throughout
the country in the weeks before Christmas.

Music, literature, art, and crafts are a vital part of
New Zealand's identity, showing through the various
media something of the country's history and diverse
cultures. New Zealand has its own opera company,
Symphony Orchestra, and Royal Ballet, with more
modest organizations operating regionally.

Since the 1970s art galleries and theaters have
increased considerably, as have awards for artistic
achievement and grants for new talent. Art in New
Zealand is diverse, with the accent on innovation
and craftsmanship reflecting the mixed heritage
of Pakeha, Maori, and Polynesian. The country's
newest museum, Te Papa, in Wellington, was built
to preserve the cultural heritage and knowledge
of the natural environment, and hosts a wealth of
exhibits in an area the size of three rugby fields. The
Dunedin Art Gallery is the oldest of its kind, and
one of the best. Even smaller towns have regular
art festivals where local artists are encouraged to
exhibit. Regular festivals feature everything from
film to chamber music, the best-known being the

country's International Arts Festival in Wellington, which began in 1984. It also has a Summer City program in January and February.

Many New Zealander artists are internationally renowned—the opera singer Kiri Te Kanawa, painters Frances Hodgkins and Colin McCahon, and composer Douglas Lilburn—and the arts can be seen around the world at major cultural events. The cabaret singer-dancer Mika, with his dance company Torotoro, performs worldwide and has appeared at the Edinburgh Festival on seven occasions.

Writing is important, with experiences from both settler and Maori life contributing to the development of New Zealand's rich native literature. Maori have been particularly prolific in this area, as storytelling is central to their culture. Poetry in song form was published in collections, one of note being the *Nga moteatea*, which was compiled by Apirana Ngata. The poet Hone Tuwhare and the novelist Witi

Ihimaera both write in English. The short-story writer Katherine Mansfield is world renowned, as well as poets Fleur Adcock, Bill Manhire, and Brian Turner; novelists Janet Frame, Maurice Gee, Keri Hulme, AlbertWendt, and detective writer Ngaio Marsh.

Man Booker Prize winners have been Keri Hulme for *The Bone People* in 1985; Lloyd Jones for *Mister Pip* in 2007;

and Eleanor Catton with *The Luminaries* in 2013, a thrilling evocation of the shenanigans on the New Zealand goldfields in the nineteenth century.

There has long been an energetic pop music scene, led by groups such as Split Enz, Crowded House, Flight of the Conchords, and Straitjacket Fits.

Film

Sir Peter Jackson's *Lord of the Rings* trilogy and the *Hobbit* trilogy have really put New Zealand on the map. Prior to that, films such as Jane Campion's *The Piano*, Lee Tamahori's *Once Were Warriors*, and *Whale Rider* have shown the extent of talent in the country, so it was just a matter of time before the industry took off from the slow beginnings of talking pictures in 1920. Initially, the emphasis was on documentary films, and few feature films were made before the 1970s. The advent of the New Zealand Film Commission, instituted in 1978, assisted filmmakers financially and the 1980s saw the industry boom. *The Return of the King* grossed $1 billion at the box office in the fastest time to date, and won Oscars in all the eleven categories for which it was nominated.

Actors Sam Neill, Anna Paquin, Rhys Darby, and Kerry Fox are well-known internationally, as is Russell Crowe, who was born in the country, but is also claimed by Australia.

Watching films is a favorite pastime whether at the cinema, on DVD, or streaming off the Internet. There are regular film festivals and film societies in the major centers. The New Zealand International Film Festival is held annually, in the latter part of the year, across the whole country.

SPORTS

Sports are a vital part of Kiwi life, and the temperate climate contributes to this. It is estimated that 74 percent of New Zealanders are active sporting enthusiasts, devoting, on average, 2.5 hours per week to physical activity. This is probably not surprising, considering their pioneering past, where the emphasis was on the physical—a great deal of time was spent clearing forests, cutting down trees, farming, and developing the land. Kiwis spend over NZ $900 million per annum on sporting activities, and related equipment and services, which represents 2.4 percent of household spending and is big business for the country. It helps that sports and recreation are well funded by government, which has provided millions for sports coordinators in secondary schools.

One-fifth of adults and one-third of children ages five to seventeen are involved with sports clubs. They are keen spectators, too, and any month will see 83 percent of adults, with 90 percent of these men, watching sports on television. Women too will get up at unearthly hours to cheer their country on in international competitions. Kiwis often get together to watch a big match on TV, particularly rugby, and you may find yourself being invited to join them, especially if you hail from the opposing country. Good-natured teasing and an essence of fair play can be expected from any such get-together, and Kiwis will always appreciate input and some general knowledge from you. Discussing sports, be it in a social or a business environment, is something of an ice-breaker, and due respect will be shown if you have something interesting to contribute. It should be noted that more than one-third of the adult population will attend a game, which is more people than go to the movies, so get yourself informed on the big game that happened last week, last night, or whenever, even if it's not your bag. Kiwis will like the fact that you bother to show interest.

A God Called Rugby

Although it is not just about rugby, it nearly is! The Russian tennis star Anna Kournikova did not score many points when she arrived in the country and was asked what she thought of the All Blacks: "What's that?" she asked; and "Who's he?" about Jonah Lomu. Rugby Union was introduced into New Zealand by the British and is firmly established as the country's national game. The country goes into mourning when the All Blacks lose, and aren't much better when any

of their other teams are in a similar boat. Today, 11 percent of adult males play and women too; the women's team, the Black Ferns won the Women's World Cup in 1998, 2002, 2006, and 2010. Other team names to know include Black Caps (cricket), Silver Ferns (netball—originally known as "women's basketball"), Black Stix (hockey), and Tall Blacks (basketball). Maori and Pacific Islanders are a vital part of New Zealand rugby. The "SupeRugby" series attracts large crowds to matches. with eighteen teams from New Zealand, Australia, Argentina, Japan and South African competing for the prestigious trophy.

Touch rugby is a popular social game of running and passing, with many businesses and social clubs fielding mixed teams of men and women over summer.

Soccer is growing in popularity, particularly among boys between the ages of five and seventeen, and it is often encouraged by parents, who consider it less dangerous than rugby. This trend has been of concern to sports writers, rugby enthusiasts, and spectators, who have seen rugby fall to the country's fifth-most popular sport for males.

Fair Play!

No mention of rugby in New Zealand can be made without mention of the 1981 Springbok tour. It divided the country and is still hotly contested today. Most Kiwis disapproved of South Africa's policies on apartheid, but the Prime Minister, Robert Muldoon, refused to stop the tour, on the basis that politics had no place in sports. The situation was responsible for days of protests, police intervention, and arrests. But the event provoked an opportunity to address the issue of racism in New Zealand.

And Other Sports

Many other sports that are played in the country are of English origin. Cricket, for instance, arrived with the missionaries in the nineteenth century and is the fourth-highest participation sport, although it does not attract as many spectators as rugby does unless there are visiting international sides. The Black Caps have acquitted themselves well in the national arena, especially for such a small nation, but do not seem to get the recognition they deserve, particularly in the press, especially when compared to rugby.

Golf is a fast-growing sport, and attracts one-quarter of the population. It is the most popular sporting activity for men, and the second for women. It is not as elitist here as in some other countries as club membership and green fees are affordable. There are more than four hundred golf courses in New Zealand, which is one of the

highest, per capita, in the world. It has still not become the spectator sport that it is internationally except when visits are made by golfers such as Tiger Woods. Champion Kiwi Michael Campbell, who has made it on the world stage, has done much to raise awareness.

Tennis is another popular recreational sport for both men and women, being the second favorite for men and third for women. Tennis clubs abound throughout the country, and participants play in all kinds of weather.

Where women's sports are concerned, netball is the most popular in terms of both participation and interest, and receives extensive TV coverage. The successes of the national team the Silver Ferns, who won the netball title at the Commonwealth Games in 2006 and 2010, and the World Cup in 2003 have contributed to the sport's popularity.

Field hockey is popular with both men and women, and more recently basketball has attracted a following among teenagers and those in their early twenties. Skiing and snowboarding are great Kiwi pastimes and Queenstown in the South Island has established a worldwide reputation for its excellent snow, and is particularly popular with visiting Australian enthusiasts. The two largest of seventeen commercial skifields, Whakapapa and Turoa, are in the North Island on Mount Ruapehu, which Aucklanders and Wellingtonians favor for a weekend away during winter.

Extreme sports are popular and probably all started with bungy jumping, which is now known worldwide by all those seeking an adrenalin rush. Chris Sigglekow and A. J. Hackett are credited with inventing this sport and made their first jump off the Auckland Harbor Bridge in 1986.

Another locally invented sport (by Sir William Hamilton in 1954 for use in the fast-flowing and shallow rivers of New Zealand) is jetboating. For a thrilling adventure take a trip around the islands, particularly in the Bay of Islands or the rivers in the Queenstown area.

Olympic Sports

New Zealanders have made contributions in this area, although, as their population is so small, their successes have not been numerous. Runners John Walker and Peter Snell are still national heroes, although the first woman to win gold in track and field events, Yvette Williams, who won the long jump in 1952 and also won four Empire Games gold medals, is not so well-known. More recently success has been in windsurfing, rowing, canoeing, horseback riding, cycling, and yachting, a combination that saw New Zealand winning thirteen medals at the 2012 Olympics—six gold, two silver and five bronze—ranking it per capita way ahead of its rival Australia. New Zealand holds fourth place, Australia thirteenth, and United Kingdom

twenty-third. Ranking is calculated according to numbers of medals per one million population Yachting is probably New Zealand's most significant achievement, and is a pursuit favored by many Kiwis.

New Zealand's feat in winning the America's Cup in 1995 and retaining it in 2000 (although they lost it in 2004) rates as a great international success. Team New Zealand is a favorite challenger for the next America's Cup in Bermuda in 2017.

MAJOR EVENTS

New Zealand has a great variety of annual festivals, sporting events, concerts, and shows ranging from music and culture to wine and food, and seasonal celebrations of spring and of winter. The following is a sample of what is on offer, but ask at information centers for a list of local events, or for any shows or festivals that cater to your particular interests.

January/February: Summer city program, Wellington. Cultural festivals around the city.

February: Marlborough Wine Festival.

February (even-numbered years): New Zealand International Festival of the Arts in Wellington, national and international cultural programs and events.

March: Golden Shears Sheep-shearing contest, Masterton.

March: Pasifika Festival, Auckland celebrates the music, food, arts and dance of the Pacific Island communities.

March (every 2 years): Te Matatini National Kapa Haka Festival is the premiere indigenous cultural event in New Zealand and the world's largest celebration of Maori traditional performing arts.

March/April (every 2 years): Warbirds Over Wanaka. International Air Show.

May: Bluff Oyster and Food Festival. Kaikoura Seafest.

May–June (every 3 years): Volvo Ocean Race around the world.

September: Kauri Festival, Northland. This is a celebration that honors the *kauri* tree and all things connected with it, with a series of events held both in and outside the Dargaville area's *kauri* forests.

October: Seafest, Canterbury. A wine and food festival with ocean emphasis.

October: HSBC—coastal classic yacht race from Auckland to Russell, the biggest coastal race in New Zealand.

November: Canterbury Show Week, Christchurch. Agricultural in flavor, with family entertainment.

November: Hunter's Garden, Marlborough. New Zealand's premier gardening event.

TAKING A BREAK

Kiwis like to take vacations, so if you are visiting New Zealand at peak times, such as Christmas and Easter, then plan far ahead. Accommodation, particularly of the cheaper type, gets booked up early. You also need to take note of Kiwi holidays, such as the Queen's birthday weekend, Labour Day, Waitangi, and Anzac Day, as many people take the opportunity to turn these into long weekends if possible. Booking ahead with domestic flights and rental vehicles is also recommended for these periods.

As the winter can be wet, gray, and miserable, many New Zealanders search for warmer climes, and take off to Australia's east coast. Queensland's Gold Coast, north of Brisbane, is a favorite, as is the Sunshine Coast, where Noosa is very much the flavor of the month. There are plenty of package vacations on offer, which include flights, accommodation, and meals.

Other favorite Kiwi destinations include the many tropical islands, such as Fiji, Rarotonga in the Cook Islands, Aitutaki, and, further away, Tahiti, Vanuatu, Samoa, and Tonga.

chapter six

TRAVEL, HEALTH, & SAFETY

ARRIVING AND DEPARTING

Every person entering New Zealand must be in possession of a valid passport that does not expires for at least one month after their planned departure date. Around sixty countries are on New Zealand's visa free list, which allows their passport holders to vacation for up to three months without a visitor visa. Applicants who intend to stay in New Zealand for more than twelve months are required to complete (and submit with their application) a General Medical Certificate

and a Chest X-ray Certificate. If you are traveling to New Zealand on business and are not receiving any payment or benefit during your time there, you will need a Business Visitor Visa. Visit www. immigration.govt.nz for official information on New Zealand's visa and passport requirements.

New Zealand is dependent on agriculture and takes its biosecurity very seriously. It is not permitted to bring into the country any plants or plant products, including herbal medicines, fruit, foodstuffs, animal products, artefacts such as wooden carvings, products from endangered species, dirty sports gear, or items that have been in contact with the soil (these may be sterilized or fumigated before being returned). As for drugs, cannabis is illegal. Penalties for smuggling are high—they can run into thousands of dollars, and possibly a jail sentence. Signs all over the airport very clearly state the rules, and there are amnesty bins to dump items in before reaching customs. Should you have anything that is vacuum-packed, declare it. Declare anything if in doubt. There will usually be sniffer dogs checking the baggage. Visit www.customs.govt.nz and www.quarantine.govt.nz for the most up-to-date information on this topic.

There are items that cannot be taken out of the country; these range from concerns for endangered species and animal welfare, such as the survival of land and marine mammals. New Zealand is actively protecting its cultural heritage and as such Maori artefacts that are over fifty years old, bones, feathers, or other parts of extinct New Zealand species and any goods over fifty years old that have national, scientific, or artistic significance cannot be removed from the country.

When To Come
You can visit New Zealand all year-round, because the climate is temperate and the attractions are so varied. November through April is usually the warmer time, and these months are the most popular. The Christmas period, which coincides with the longer school vacation, is when locals take off to the beach so accommodation will be harder to come

by. February usually has the warmest and most settled weather.

There is plenty to do throughout the year, although it is advisable to book ahead if you are going during peak times. There are activities such as bungy jumping, tramping (hiking) or cycling, skiing, fishing, and swimming with dolphinsfor the more adventurous, and wine tasting, whale watching, and plain sightseeing for others. New Zealand offers excellent and varied skiing and boarding, of course, in the winter months from June to August. Visit www.newzealandski.co.nz for the best information on where and when to ski.

As far as clothes go, the most sensible idea is layers; bring things that you can put on or peel off, such as T-shirts, jerseys, and jackets. Don't forget rainwear, as you will surely need it at some time or other on your trip.

GETTING AROUND

As New Zealand is not a large country, especially when compared to its Tasman neighbor, and travel within the country is relatively easy, inexpensive, and efficient.

Flying

Air travel over longer distances has replaced buses and trains, but that depends on whether you want a rapid bird's-eye view or a more leisurely scenic journey. Besides Auckland and Wellington, there are international airports at Christchurch, Dunedin, Hamilton, Palmerston North, and Queenstown, and at around twenty smaller towns like Kerikeri

and Wanganui. Some of the small airlines have been grouped under the country's main airline, Air New Zealand, to form "Air New Zealand Link," which practically covers the country. Besides Air New Zealand, which charges more for flights if a foreign card is used, there are cheaper alternatives such as Jet Star and Qantas. Budget fares are usually available the further ahead you book, especially if done electronically. Most airlines offer electronic ticketing, which, by Internet, is cheaper and often more convenient than over-the-counter purchases.

Buses

There is an extensive bus/coach network over each island—Intercity operates New Zealand's largest passenger transport network across both—while there are local companies specific to various areas. Services between the main cities usually operate several times a day and throughout the week.

There are also shuttle services, operated by smaller companies, and some geared especially to overseas visitors and backpackers. They are also a good alternative for traveling into the city from airports. Kiwi Experience offers all-in-one package tours which allow you to get on and off where you please.

Buses are reliable and comfortable, and usually run on time, but there can be congestion on weekends, especially when leaving major centers on a Friday afternoon and arriving back on Sunday evening. Travel can be much slower, on long weekends and peak seasonal times.

North of Auckland there is only one major road out of the city, which forks to follow the west coast via Dargaville or goes straight on to Paihia and the Bay of Islands. Similarly in the South Island, roads are few because of the vast mountain range. Roads traveling from east to west are also few because of the topographical challenges the country presents.

Most roads in New Zealand, while scenic, are narrow and winding, so traveling can be slow and tiring.

Trains

There are not so many train routes, although train travel is reasonably fast and a good way to see the country. Rating among the spectacular train journeys of the world are the Coastal Pacific from Christchurch to Picton, which runs along the South Island's rugged northeast coast and the TranzAlpine from Christchurch to Greymouth, which passes through magnificent mountain scenery. Intercity rail services are operated by Tranz Scenic, but there are a number of other train routes such as the Northern Explorer, between Auckland and Wellington, and the Capital Connection, from Palmerston North to Wellington. It has taken over seventy years for trains to return to the center of Auckland, following years of political wrangling and

muddle, mainly because the route went through contested Maori land. The city is constructing an underground railway—"City Rail Link—in the central business district to ease city congestion.

Ferries and Boats

The Bluebridge and Interislander ferry services operate between the North and South Islands (Wellington and Picton), although these are cancelled if the sea is too rough, and then you take the plane! There are also passenger and car ferry services operating between Auckland and Waiheke and Auckland and Great Barrier Island in the Hauraki Gulf, and passenger ferry services between Bluff and Stewart Island. Smaller local car ferry services operate in Northland across the Hokianga Harbors and in the Bay of Islands. Off the Bay of Islands there are trips out to sea and around the islands—this is a real must—and there are also

trips on the various lakes and around the Fiordland area of the South Island. Commuter ferries operate in Auckland and Wellington. For thrill seekers, the New Zealand–designed jet boat offers an unforgettable river travel experience. Information can be found at www.river. jet.co.nz.

Car Rental

Car rental is available at all the major airports and can be booked on the Internet, with special deals available. Many people rent motor homes or campers, as one does not always have to stay at official camping sites, and this makes some of the most inaccessible places available to intrepid travelers.

You can legally drive in New Zealand for up to 12 months if you have either a current driver's license from your home country, or an International Driving Permit (IDP). All drivers, including overseas visitors, must carry their license or permit when driving. You will only be able to drive the same types of vehicles you are licensed to drive in your home country. The common legal age to rent a car in New Zealand is 25 years. If your licence is not in English, you should be able to provide an official translation. As a visiting, driver you need to be aware of New Zealand's traffic law and safe driving practices. Visit www.nzta.govt. nz for the official road code. In New Zealand, all motorists drive on the left-hand side of the road. The speed limit on the open road is 100 kilometres per hour (approximately 60 miles per hour) and 50 kilometres per hour in built-up areas. Drivers and passengers must wear seat belts at all times.

Drinking and driving is a serious offense. The rules are strictly enforced, and police carry out breath-test blitzes on expressways and elsewhere, using blood tests where necessary. Kiwis are, by and large, law-abiding, and do not run the risk of over-imbibing and driving. They will either use taxis, which are expensive, or agree on one nondrinker in the party as the driver for the evening.

Don't use any "I'm a visitor/foreigner and did not know the law/see the sign" excuses for speeding offenses, as police have no discretion, and vehicles that exceed the speed limit by more than 6 mph (10 kmph) are automatically ticketed. Fixed and mobile cameras (often in police cars) are used anywhere and at any time.

Cycling

New Zealand is rich in breathtaking scenery and cycling around the country is a rewarding way to

appreciate the country. It is a cheap form of travel favored by many, both because it is clean and green, and because of the clear, uncrowded roads. There are 23 Great Rides that make up the New Zealand Cycle Trail that covers both islands. Renting a bike is easy and plenty of rental providers can be found in the main centers around the trails of each of the Great Rides. Visit www. nzcycletrail.com for a comprehensive list of trails.

Wearing a helmet is mandatory, as it is for motorcyclists. If you're cycling on the road, you must know New Zealand's road rules. *The Official New Zealand Code for Cyclists*, developed by the New Zealand Transport Agency, is a user-friendly guide to New Zealand's traffic laws and safe driving practices.

FACILITIES FOR THE DISABLED

In New Zealand, by law, every new building and major reconstruction must provide "reasonable and adequate" access for people with disabilities.

All larger accommodations provide rooms suitable for visitors with limited mobility. Tour operators such as Ability Adventures and Accessible Kiwi Tours can provide advice to travelers and holiday packages for individuals and groups. Most transport operators do cater for people with special needs, but it is recommended to phone ahead to check availability. Some urban transport buses are equipped to cater for the disabled, and they are marked on the outside of the bus. Companies that offer cars with hand controls include Budget and Freedom Mobility.

Booking ahead is recommended. More information on accessible transport is available on weka.net.nz.

Throughout the country there are designated parking areas for the disabled. Parking concessions are available for people with disabilities, and temporary display cards can be issued for the length of a visitor's stay. Disability parking permits issued in other countries do not automatically work in New Zealand. To get a New Zealand mobility parking permit you will need to show your home mobility card or a medical certificate as proof of disability.

WHERE TO STAY

There are approximately four thousand establishments offering accommodation throughout the country. Motels are the popular choice for most visitors. They are usually self-catering, but some offer breakfast and dinner and have a restaurant on site. Bed and breakfast accommodation and more expensive hotels can all be found on sites such as www.aatravel.co.nz and www.jasons.co.nz. These can be booked and paid for in advance. Home and farmstays (www.truenz.co.nz/farmstays) are also popular with visitors.

Backpacking accommodation is available everywhere, sometimes at attractive sites and in older buildings (www.bbh.co.nz), and there are many youth hostels (www.yha.org.nz).

There are commercial camping grounds throughout the country, and camping sites in all

the national parks, as well as huts for which a permit needs to be obtained. Kiwis believe that fabulous views and desirable destinations should not be the prerogative of the rich, so camping and caravan parks are often situated in prime areas.

HEALTH AND SAFETY

New Zealand is generally a very safe place to travel with a relatively low crime rate; however, visitors are still advised to take the same care with their personal safety and possessions as they would in any other country. Copies of important documents such as passport and credit cards should be carried and kept separate from the originals, so too a record of the description and serial number of cameras, tablets, and smart phones.

It is a very benign country. There are no dangerous animals, and possibly the worst offender is the *katipo* spider, which is only found in grasses above beaches,

STAYING SAFE IN THE OUTDOORS

Most visitors come to New Zealand to enjoy the outstanding natural environment but there are precautions that should be taken. Firstly, take the time to learn about where you are going and to seek advice from your local i-SITE or Department of Conservation (DOC) Visitor Center on how to be best prepared.

Cell phone: Coverage is unreliable outside the main city centers and if you are venturing into the bush or the mountains you are unlikely to get reception. Consider carrying a personal locator beacon and a battery powered radio, especially if you're traveling alone.

Weather: It can be very variable and severe at times. Always be prepared for wet, cold weather and on days when it is sunny, remember that New Zealand's clear, unpolluted atmosphere and relatively low latitudes produce sunlight that is stronger than in much of Europe or North America, so be prepared to wear a hat and use sunblock. Always check the weather forecast and be prepared for four seasons in one day. Check weather conditions and any alerts issued by the Parks and Recreation (DOC) before you set out. Treat all weather warnings seriously.

Challenging terrain: Don't underestimate any "walk" outside the main centers. You need to be reasonably fit. Check out the recommended level of fitness required for any walk before you head off. You also need the right clothing and proper footwear. City daywear will not be suitable.

Tell someone where you are going: Tell someone your plans and leave a date for when to raise the alarm if you haven't returned. Leave a detailed trip plan with the Department of Conservation (DOC) or a friend, including a "panic" date. The more details there are about your intentions, the quicker you'll be rescued if something goes wrong. You can find a handy Outdoor Intentions form on the www.adventuresmart.org.nz

and whose bite can be painful and lead to heart palpitations. It has now become endangered and is rare in dunes close to human habitation, so you would be very unlucky to encounter it. Shark attacks are rare, and the many species in waters off the coast probably have more to fear from humans.

More to the point is the hole in the ozone layer. In 2003 a record loss of 47.3 million tons of ozone occurred, which is equivalent to around 17.5 lbs (around 8 kilograms) of ozone per person. The hole breaks up over Antarctica and moves over New Zealand and the southern hemisphere at the end of November and in early December, when extreme levels of UV radiation levels occur. It is essential to use a sunblock with a high UV factor when venturing outside, and as a general rule, the sun should be avoided between 11:00 a.m. and 3:00 p.m. A sun hat and sunglasses should always be worn in direct sunlight. Radio and TV weather forecasters usually incorporate a "burn factor" (the amount of time one can stay in the sun without incurring sunburn) in their daily news reports. Melanoma kills almost one New Zealander a day!

Should you require health care while in the country, visiting a local doctor or dentist will cost NZ $50 on average and, while the New Zealand hospital system is free to its citizens, foreign nationals are charged for treatment, except immediately following an accident, so it is important to have comprehensive travel insurance.

One-quarter of New Zealanders over the age of fifteen smoke, and all packets of cigarettes carry health warnings—in Maori as well, as many more Maori New Zealanders smoke. New Zealand is actively considering introducing plain packaging laws and is closely following the results of its introduction in Australia. Cancer has been the main cause of death for over ten years, followed by heart and cerebrovascular disease, and there has been a reemergence of tuberculosis among Pacific Islanders, while diabetes is also significant.

CRIME

Although crime is increasing in New Zealand, it has a long way to go to catch up with the rest of the world. In the smaller, remoter towns, children leave their bicycles in a hedge for the day before catching the school bus, and pick them up in the afternoons; vegetables, fruit, and other items are left out by the grower next to an honesty box for payment, and at home keys are left under the mat for visitors, or the back door is left unlocked. Sadly, there are always those who take advantage, and theft is the most frequent crime, with theft from cars increasing, particularly in the larger cities like Auckland—so don't leave items on display, and keep valuables locked in the trunk (boot). In general, take normal safety precautions with your possessions, and keep documents such as passports locked up in hotel rooms or in a secure place.

Although the number of murders has not, to date, exceeded one hundred annually, violence in general is on the increase, especially grievous bodily harm and other assaults. As much of this is associated with alcohol, it is advisable to avoid rowdy downtown bars late in the evening. You can safely walk around city centers at night, although in the larger cities there are some "no-go" areas, which you would do well to check on and avoid.

The national police force is generally polite, patient, and helpful. Policemen carry batons, tasers, and OC spray (pepper spray) rather than firearms, so are not as intimidating as those you meet elsewhere in the world; however, they do not hesitate to act should the occasion warrant. They are trained to handle firearms for use in specific circumstances. Police officers working at international airports or part of the Diplomatic Protection Sqaud are armed.

BUSINESS BRIEFING

GENERAL ATTITUDE TO BUSINESS

The average New Zealander shies away from discussing business issues or the economy, probably because these are, on the whole, not well understood. Surveys also note that this lack of business interest or literacy is reflected in the low readership of business-oriented media. It is not surprising, therefore, that for Kiwis business success is not high on the

esteem agenda. This is possibly a spillover of the "tall poppy" syndrome, it being considered that successful businessmen should be modest about their talents and hide them under a bushel. This said, certain Kiwi business successes, such as The Warehouse's Sir Stephen Tindall, are often admired, although the fact that he started up on his own from scratch and is also involved in socially responsible projects is probably significant. Because the importance of business to the economy is not generally recognized, particularly the connection between a strong economy and the social well-being of the country, it is not surprising that there are moves afoot to promote a positive attitude to business and to create a business-friendly environment, so that Kiwis will make the connection between good economic growth and a high standard of living, to which they all aspire.

THE KIWI WORKPLACE
Environment
The New Zealand work environment is no different in atmosphere from other sectors and is generally informal and laid-back. They have adopted a good life/work balance. Most New Zealanders are friendly, obliging, and courteous, and expect a similar attitude from you. Rude or demanding behavior at any level falls on deaf ears or invokes blank stares. Status, rank, and hierarchy are much less important in Kiwi workplaces than elsewhere in the world. Staff is respectful of its managers, but they are seen as one of the team. Management style is usually informal, and so

is the workplace. Superiors, colleagues, and clients are usually addressed by their first names. Dress is quite casual.

The Workforce

New Zealanders have a strong independent and egalitarian streak that affects the way they like to work and be managed. A top-down management approach is not popular and it is expected that everyone will contribute in a team-like fashion. Businesses generally are smaller, often employing fewer than twenty people and being able to work in a team is highly valued. New Zealanders are known for getting "stuck in" and finding solutions.

Approximately two-thirds of adults are in the workforce, with three-quarters of these working full-time. The number of part-time workers, especially female, has increased greatly. Don't be surprised to find your counterpart is female, as women hold most of the top jobs in the country. This is a very egalitarian society, where women are considered equal to men. However, according to NZX Diversity statistics for 2015, women made up just 17 percent of directors and 19 percent of senior management in publicly listed companies. Despite the Equal Pay Act of 1972 that made different pay rates illegal, there remains a persistent pay gap. In 2014 New Zealand was 33rd of 142 countries in the *World Economic Forum* Global Gender Gap Report rankings of wage equality for similar work. In New Zealand, the gender pay gap is significantly influenced by ethnicity.

The public sector employs 18 percent of the workforce. This figure is low by world standards, but is partly due to the sale of several government concerns in the 1980s when it was nearer 25 percent.

Changes in the economy have led to more people being employed in the services sector, with over 27 percent employed in community, social, and personal services, followed by nearly 23 percent in the wholesale and retail trade, restaurants, and hotels. Manufacturing accounts for only 12 percent. In December 2015 New Zealand's unemployment rate was 5.3 percent while the labor force participation rate had reached a record 69.7 percent. On average, the labor force has become better educated and more skilled.

Approximately 16 percent of the workforce is unionized, there being, in 2013, approximately 138 unions. Early last century New Zealand was one of the most unionized countries in the world. Membership has fallen considerably since 1989, when 47 percent of the workforce belonged to a trade union, largely due to an act of 1991, which stripped union privileges and encouraged individual contracts. A subsequent act in 2000 required employers, workers, and unions to deal with each other openly and honestly.

LEGISLATION

New Zealand has a great deal of legislation concerning employment. All employees are entitled to a minimum wage, annual leave, and public holidays.

There are also entitlements to sick and bereavement leave, arrangements for those working on Public Holidays, and directions as to calculating holiday pay. All employees are entitled to a minimum of four weeks' annual leave as well as the eleven paid public holidays.

Parental leave is available to both partners around the birth of a child, and to those adopting a child under the age of five. Employees must have worked for at least twelve months, with an average of ten hours a week prior to the anticipated date of birth. In April 2016 paid leave was increased to eighteen weeks, with another ten days available during pregnancy for related reasons, and paternity leave amounts to two weeks. Extended leave is also available up to twelve months, and this may be taken by either parent, or shared, with maternity leave being deducted from the total.

WORKING IN NEW ZEALAND

To work in New Zealand, one needs to be a citizen or permanent resident, or to have a work permit or appropriate visa, which should be applied for in advance. Casual jobs, particularly in agriculture, such as fruit picking, are obtainable by visitors (check out picknz.co.nz). The New Zealand Working Holiday Scheme (WHS) work permit or work visa allows you to be in New Zealand for up to 12 months (or 23 months for Canadian or British passport holders), and to work for up to three months for any one employer. If you choose to lengthen your stay, be warned that staying more than 183 days in a twelve-month period means that New Zealand's Inland Revenue could tax your worldwide income. The country has double taxation agreements with several countries to avoid tax being paid twice. To know where you stand, check out www.ird.govt.nz.

DOING BUSINESS IN NEW ZEALAND
New Zealand has a relatively deregulated, open economy and is recognized globally as being a safe place to invest and do business. A nation with a high level of economic freedom and one of the least corrupt, it is consistently ranked as one of the easiest countries in which to do business. It has a straightforward, business-friendly taxation system that supports capital development, research and development, and international investment.

MAKING APPOINTMENTS
Personal connections are important for visiting businessmen and women, and it is probably easier to schedule a meeting with senior-level management through a contact, but if this is not possible plan well in advance. Don't just show up—make an appointment, and expect to have to wait a few days for a response. Identifying the right person to deal with will probably happen faster if you explain your requirements, that you are a visitor, and that you need help. Kiwis like to be helpful, and will readily respond to such a request. Be aware that key personnel may be away during school holidays, especially in the prime summer vacations and Easter.

MEETINGS

Be on time, as arriving late may give the impression that you are not reliable or, even worse, think yourself slightly superior to your counterpart by indicating your time is more valuable.

Depending on the type of business, suits and ties are usually worn although, for future meetings, you can take your lead from your counterpart's attire and dress accordingly. For women, a suit or smart dress is appropriate. Advertising, the media in general, publishing, the computer industry, and other related creative businesses are usually more informal.

Meetings are usually relaxed and friendly. You will be on first-name terms from the start, and it is acceptable to stand or sit in a relaxed manner as formality is not important to the average Kiwi. However, don't misinterpret this. Being too forward or overly friendly won't be appreciated—this is a business environment, after all. Professionalism, integrity, and a straightforward approach are important characteristics to display. A certain amount of small talk can be expected before getting down to business, and this is where knowledge of the latest happenings in New Zealand, such as last week's rugby game, is helpful—even the weather will do!

Their informality sometimes means that meetings may be extended to include lunch or dinner.

PRESENTATIONS

If a presentation is required, stick to facts and figures and avoid exaggeration and hype. Kiwis appreciate openness, honesty, and directness, and need down-to-earth observations and comments rather than bells and whistles. Some history of your product or service, testimonials, and references will be expected, as well as your showing knowledge and understanding of relevant local conditions such as customs requirements, government regulations, and industrial relations, so do your homework before you come. The New Zealand Embassy, Consulate, or Trade Attaché in your own country will be able to supply appropriate information and clarify what is expected and what is appropriate.

A few questions from you will not go amiss, as you cannot be expected to know everything. When giving a presentation, be sure to maintain eye contact and respect personal space. Some humor is always a good idea, and is usually an icebreaker. Don't use slang or profanity, as you will lose respect, or discuss issues of a sensitive nature such as race, feminism, and immigration, unless your counterpart raises such a topic.

NEGOTIATING

Kiwis should not be hurried during the negotiating or decision-making process. They will not appreciate numerous follow-up calls, high-pressure sales tactics, close deadlines, or the like. Be aware, too, that they are not always diligent about returning calls. You should demonstrate a product's capability rather than talk about it, and don't oversell (as that can lead to overkill). New Zealanders will make their own judgment and won't trust you if they think you are exaggerating or making extravagant claims. Stick to the point and do not impart more detail than necessary. Brevity is appreciated. However, don't skimp on explaining terms and conditions, and be sure you have included everything. With regard to costs, be realistic and don't complicate matters by offering discounts and cut-rate deals, especially if these are given to exact an immediate order. New Zealanders do not expect to haggle over prices, as this is not their culture, but they do look for a fair cost and value for money. Be concise, straightforward, honest, and direct. It is also important that you stick to your undertakings and do not make promises you cannot keep. Kiwis are very trusting until they are given a reason not to be. It is difficult to heal a broken business relationship, and future dealings will undoubtedly be impaired or could even cease altogether. However, if you do build up a good business relationship, it will be worthwhile, as New Zealanders are loyal and fair.

CONTRACTS

Shake hands on a deal, but get it down on paper to ensure there are no misunderstandings. Like many people, Kiwis have been known to change their minds or rethink quotes, and do not always abide by their decisions. A contract needs to be attentive to detail, and matters should be spelled out if there is any doubt. Kiwis can vary from being very pedantic in pointing out certain discrepancies to not noticing major howlers, so be prepared for all contingencies, and check.

RESOLVING DISPUTES

New Zealand is not a litigious society, and you would have to be very unfortunate if a dispute arose and legal recourse were the only option. Kiwis, by and large, do not like confrontation, and would make a big effort to avoid this. However, if there is disagreement then tackle it—don't beat around the bush—and look at the options. You will usually find that something can be worked out, and you should get their commitment to solving the problem before looking at possible ways of doing so. Mediation, with the use of facilitators, is becoming a more popular alternative than resorting to law because it is less costly, not only in monetary terms but in terms of time and psychological stress.

chapter **eight**

COMMUNICATING

UNDERSTANDING THE "LINGO"

While New Zealanders speak English, it is a particular
brand of English, commonly called Newzild or
Kiwinglish in New Zealand, involving some differences
of vocabulary and accent. Identifying characteristics are
flattened vowel sounds and a certain nasal intonation.
It is a good idea not to muddle the Kiwi accent with
the Australian one, however similar you think the two
may be! Rather ask whereabouts a person is from, and
if the response is "New Zealand," it's a good idea to
reply that you knew that (which will score you some
points)—what you meant was which town! Sydney is
pronounced "Seedney" by Aussies and "Sudney" by
Kiwis. Possibly even better as an example is "feesh en
cheeps" by Aussies and "fush un chups" by Kiwis. If you
can pick up these subtleties, you are doing well. Both
accents carry a rising inflection at the end of a sentence,
which seems to turn everything into a question.
Visitors are often unsure as to whether an answer of
some sort is then required from them, particularly
if they first asked a question. Sometimes it does not
inspire a lot of confidence in the answer, especially
if you are asking directions. Attentive listening and

nods will normally do the trick and repetition of the information just given. Even then you could get "Yep" or "I reckon" as your confirmation that you have got it right.

A survey not so long ago revealed that Kiwis, by and large, do not like their own accent, considering it inferior to an English accent and even to an American. It is interesting to note that the *Reed Dictionary of New Zealand English* includes meanings and pronunciations peculiar to New Zealand. Any library will have one, and it may be worth your while to glance through it. For instance, words like "four" or "door" are pronounced as if they have two syllables "four-a" and "door-a." Check out, too, *The New Zealand Dictionary*, which goes one step further, recognizing that New Zealand has its own variety of English. It contains lots of typical Kiwi words and phrases, such as the response sometimes given when you ask someone if he is well: "Box of birds" could be the retort (which makes a change from "good"). This means that he's very well, although the Kiwi dictionary says it means "success," probably harking back to the days of shooting for the pot. You may see a sign on expressways inviting you to "dob in" (inform on) anyone committing the offenses of bad driving, speeding, or other violations. When joining from a side road you will see signs urging you to "merge like a zip."

If you plan to stay in the country for a while, and maybe consider renting or even buying a home, then a whole new vocabulary is necessary. For instance, if you prefer the countryside to live in, refer to it as the "wopwops," or even "backblocks," which is a term originally given to land bought from Maori but that came to mean "more remote farming." A piece of land is called a "block." Asking for a "plot" will result in your being shown the nearest cemetery! If requiring something a little bigger than a "block," then "section" or "lifestyle block" are the terms.

There has been a significant uptake of indigenous words and phrases from the Maori language. It was actively suppressed for many years

after colonization; however, today there are as many as 1,000 Maori words used regularly by non-native speakers. Words like *waka* (technically canoe, but often used to describe any motor vehicle), *kia ora* (hello), *kai* (food), *puku* (belly, stomach), and *whanau* (family) can now be heard interspersed in everyday Kiwi conversation.

The Maori language is evident in more than just spoken, colloquial language. It is becoming part of the language of NZ officialdom. Take *tangata whenua* (people of the land) and *iwi* (tribe) for example. They're now commonly used in the press and, importantly, in legislation, without an accompanying English translation.

KIWI COMMUNICATION STYLES

As we have seen, the Kiwis are generally unpretentious, informal, and down to earth, and prefer it if you adopt a similar approach. You are not expected to prove yourself in any way, and will be taken at face value. Too much directness can be seen as aggression, so it is wise to tread warily, and watch your ps and qs until you are better acquainted. Similarly, go easy on questions, as this can seem like an inquisition, and Kiwis will back off, but simple inquiries about the country, the way of life, and other related topics, that stem from interest rather than seeming to come from a checklist, will be met with polite answers.

Too much familiarity is not appreciated, at least initially. Kiwis are not backslapping, "hail fellow well-met" types, and it is important to respect personal space—an arm's length is probably adequate. A simple handshake will do, although once you get to know a Kiwi you can expect a friendly pat on the back, or something similar

The usual greeting, "How are ya," is often rolled into one word, and a response is not expected, so don't launch into any kind of description of how you are! Kiwis often deliver this greeting to strangers, for instance while out walking, and it is probably the equivalent of "Morning!" In this context a simple smile or nod of recognition will do—that's if they've bothered to make eye contact in the first place, which they often don't. If somebody is really asking you how you are, the traditional response is, "Good, thanks." Now adopted by many Kiwis, but previously just a

Maori custom, is a raising of the eyebrows as an informal acknowledgment of your presence after eye contact has been made.

Kiwis are happy to receive compliments, so feel free to admire their homes, decor, possessions, and so on, especially as an icebreaker. It is a good idea, when you are invited into a house, to offer to remove your shoes before entering; many do so to protect floor coverings.

"No-nos"

Swearing is no longer uncommon as it was fifty years ago; it has become part of the everyday conversation. However, the "f—" word is frowned on, although it may be used in informal, casual environments. Getting drunk in public is also considered offensive, and Kiwis are usually careful about their drinking and driving, as being stopped by the law and found guilty leads to an endorsement on your driver's license. The general attitude to drunkenness is becoming more relaxed—it's all right if it happens now and again—although there is concern about the increase in drinking among teenagers.

Be careful about gestures, as what means something in one society is often not the same in another, George Bush's flashing what he thought was the **V** for Victory sign to Australians being a case in point. Don't forget that the *marae* (meeting ground) is considered sacrosanct by the Maori, and be guided by New Zealanders when on a visit. Be aware that Polynesians are humble and modest, and do not engage in prolonged eye contact. Similarly,

SOME DOS AND DON'TS

- Do praise the country.
- Do enthuse about all things New Zealand.
- Do appreciate their sporting achievements, particularly in rugby and sailing, and, when in a female environment, netball!
- Do make an effort to understand rugby.
- Do talk about the weather.
- Do learn a few Maori words.
- Do respect Maori customs.
- Do tell jokes about yourself and the Australians.
- Don't confuse them with Australians.
- Don't even mention the word "convict." New Zealand was never a penal colony.
- Don't criticize.
- Don't advise how to do things better.
- Don't moan about the weather.
- Don't make suggestions until you really know what you're talking about.
- Don't present too many new-fangled ideas.
- Don't suggest that where you come from things are done differently or better.
- Don't make comments implying that New Zealand is "not in the world."
- Don't take photos of people, particularly Maoris and Polynesians, without asking.

ensure that you do not sit higher than a Polynesian counterpart, as this is considered rude.

USE OF HUMOR

Kiwis usually have a quiet sense of humor, and always appreciate a conversation that has tongue-in-cheek comments or the odd joke or two, particularly if the flavor is of a self-deprecating nature, or anti-Australian! Gauge the sensitivity of the recipients of jokes you may feel inclined to tell, as humor in New Zealand varies throughout the country and can range from being so subtle as to be obscure to much more obvious.

MAIL SERVICES

Always regarded as efficient and reliable, but as customers are increasingly turning to electronic communication the New Zealand postal service has reduced its standard six-day-a-week delivery service to just three days. The alternative but almost twice as expensive is FastPost. It has a next working day delivery target for sending across town or between major towns and cities and offers a range of letter sizes and postage options. The required postage is based on the size and weight of your letter or document. Post shops are in every town, sometimes incorporated into another shop like a bookshop, but will have the recognizable sign outside. They are open every day except Saturday afternoons and Sundays.

Courier services offer either urgent overnight or economy deliveries, and a track and trace service provides the opportunity to check on an item at any time from pick-up to delivery.

There are several overseas mail services. International Express is a track and trace courier service covering more than 220 countries for delivery within days, and to Australian centers the next morning. International Air delivers in one to two weeks with track and trace facilities to certain countries, and International Economy within three to five weeks.

A Poste Restante, or mail holding service, is available at bigger post offices in cities. Mail will be held for up to three months, free of charge, although parcels may be subject to a storage fee when collected. For further information check www.nzpost.com.

MODERN TECHNOLOGY

Rapid expansion in communication technology, especially with the increased use of computers and the Internet, mobile, and digital technology, has affected the more traditional methods, such as telephone and fax, particularly in a small country like New Zealand. Kiwis are not only technologically aware but realistic about their geographical isolation, and the Internet has been a boon in countering this with more that 86 percent of the population being regular users. Most Kiwis are completely *au fait* with such activities as e-mail, EFTPOS transactions, automatic teller machines, Internet banking, cell phones and text messaging, and digital cameras.

Eighty percent of all Kiwi homes have at least one computer. Internet access is not expensive, and this factor has contributed to its rapid expansion. There are some 80 Internet Service Providers servicing 1,916,000 broadband connections and 65,000 dialup connections.

Telephones, Cell Phones, and Internet

In 2012 New Zealand had 4,922,000 cell phones in use, several hundred thousand more than its population, ranking it in fifty-ninth place on the list of number of cell phones in use per country.

If you need to be connected to the Internet when in New Zealand, it's recommended that you purchase a plan from one of New Zealand's main networks: Vodafone, 2degrees, Spark and Skinny. Free Wi-Fi hotspots are generally found in main cities only. Buying a plan from one of the networks

USEFUL TELEPHONE NUMBERS

111 Emergency number for all services. You will be directed to Police, Fire, or Ambulance on request.

*555 Mobile telephone number to report nonemergency traffic incidents such as a breakdown, car crash with no injuries, road hazard

018 National Directory Assistance

0172 International Directory Inquiries

Numbers in New Zealand can be found on the Internet using www.whitepages.co.nz

will allow you to have access to a mix of data, calling, and texting.

There are not that many public phones, but they can usually be found in areas such as airports and shopping centers. These mostly use a local telephone prepaid card and coins, but some will accept credit cards. Prepaid cards are available from bookstores, supermarkets, and service stations. New Zealand phone numbers can be found online in the White Pages (alphabetical listings, including business and residential) and Yellow Pages (business category listings).

CONCLUSION

New Zealand is a long way from most other countries in the world—but it is well worth the journey. It is a country of beauty, charm, and great diversity. Because it is not quite "in the world," it is a very relaxing place to visit. The time zone usually means that people are rising just when much of the world is going to sleep, and vice versa, which can make international communication a bit irksome. The Kiwis are used to this, just as they are used to being far from anywhere and anything, which can have its advantages—9/11 being a case in point.

The wine is internationally renowned, the beer good, and the food of such variety that boredom is not an option. There's a lot to see, and a multitude of activities at all times of the year.

The people of New Zealand are informal, nonjudgmental, friendly, and kind. From the local "postie"(mail carrier) to the man behind the counter in the dairy, to the Kiwi casually met in the street, you will find a readiness to stop and help, and direct you if you're lost—and you don't always have to ask. Looking at a map, or looking uncertain, will practically guarantee that someone will approach you and offer assistance. Similarly, because Kiwis are trusting and honest, you can leave your luggage with them for a few hours, ask them to let the electrician into the house, or even leave the key under the mat for him. That sense of wellbeing and ease doesn't happen in many places in the world today.

Further Reading

Bennett, Joe. *A Land of two Halves*. London: Scribner, 2004.

Dew, Josie. *Long Cloud Ride*. London: Sphere, 2007.

Duff, Alan. *Once Were Warriors*. New York: Vintage International, 1995.

Elder, Alexander. *Straying From the Flock: Travels in New Zealand*. Hoboken, New Jersey: John Wiley and Sons, Inc., 2005.

Harper, Laura et al. *The Rough Guide to New Zealand*. London: Rough Guides, 2004.

Hillary, Edmund. *Nothing Venture, Nothing Win*. London: Hodder and Stoughton, 1975.

Hulme, Keri. *The Bone People*. USA: Penguin non-classics, 1986. (Won the Booker Prize in 1985.)

Ihimaera, Witi. *The Whale Rider*. Auckland: Reed Publishing, 2003.

King, Michael. *Penguin History of New Zealand*. Eastbourne: Gardners Books, 2005. (Won Readers Choice award in 2004.)

King, Michael King. *Being Pakeha: An Encounter With New Zealand and the Maori Renaissance*. London: Hodder and Stoughton, 1985.

Mansfield, Katherine. *Short Stories of . . .* , New York: Ecco Press, 1983.

Moore, Bob. *The 1 Thing: A Small Epic Journey Down New Zealand's Mother Road*. Auckland: New Holland Publishers (NZ), 2006.

Patterson, John. *Exploring Maori Values*. Auckland: Dunmore Press, 1992.

Poole, Kate. *Eyewitness Travel Guides*. New York: DK Publishing, 2003.

Romanos, Joseph. *New Zealand's Top 100 History-Makers*. Wellington: Trio Books, 2005.

Sinclair, Kenneth. *A History of New Zealand*. Auckland: Pelican, 4th Rev. Ed., 1991.

Sinclair, Kenneth. *A Destiny Apart: New Zealand's Search for a National Identity*. Wellington: Allen & Unwin, 1986.

Smitz, Paul, et al. *Lonely Planet: New Zealand*. Hawthorne, Victoria; Oakland, California; London; Paris: Lonely Planet Publications, 2004.

Tarling, Nicholas. *The Essential Pocket Kiwi*. Auckland: Dunmore Press, 1995.

Thomas, Gail et al (eds). *My Home Now: Migrants and Refugees to New Zealand Tell Their Stories*. Auckland: Cape Catley, 2005.

Thompson, Christina. *Come on Shore and We Will Kill and Eat You All*. London: Bloomsbury, 2008.

culture smart! **new zealand**

Index